IT AIN'T NO DISEASE!

The Shattering Of A Myth About Alcoholism.

By Joyce Hovelsrud

ARK BOOKS
535 North 4th Street
Minneapolis, MN 55401

(Owned and operated by MIDWEST CHALLENGE, INC.)

COVER ART: Terry Dugan

ARK BOOKS
Copyright © 1978

Printed in the United States of America

Dedicated to

my daughters,
Angela and Cynthia

Table of Contents

Author's Note

Supposing God were here right now. Supposing He were to write an open letter regarding the subject of alcohol—that liquid so many millions can't go without—that liquid which affects every home in America. What do you think He would say?

I have long felt we can boldly proclaim He *is* here, He *is* speaking and He *has* addressed the subject of compulsive drinking in His Word, the Bible.* The material in this book is based on the Scriptures, and I have used the open letter format in an attempt to make God's message on the subject clear.

This letter is written to you who drink and to you who never drink. It is written to you who are looking for a way out and to you who are trying to help a loved one or friend. Read it carefully. I believe there to be truth expressed in love on every page, and that the way to freedom is made plain.

JH

---

*Verses marked TLB are taken from The Living Bible, Copyright 1971 by Tyndale House Publishers, Wheaton, Ill. Used by permission.

Introduction

We selected *It Ain't No Disease* as a title for this book not for its literary merit obviously, but rather as our way of saying may we have your attention please. We feel it has something terribly important to say.

The material contained in these pages has been written for all those who are dealing with problems of and related to habitual compulsive drinking; and we believe it contains the truth about a subject so shrouded in delusion not even the many who are involved in the treatment of those afflicted have seen it.

Exactly what *is* it that triggers a compulsion for drinking alcohol? We believe knowing the answer to that question is prerequisite to securing release from such compulsion. We believe that the One who created man in His image has addressed this problem specifically and that He answers that question in His Word.

We believe also that He has given clear and concise instructions for breaking the chains which bind men and women in those compulsions which are destructive and life-threatening, and that those who seek to know the truth will find restoration as well as freedom because the Creator guarantees it!

Written as God's open letter to the compulsive drinker and to those concerned about him, this book is based on the truth of Scripture as we perceive it to be; and it is our prayer that many will be helped by it.

The Publishers

Foreword

In my judgment such of us who have never fallen victims [of alcohol] have been spared more by the absence of appetite than from any mental or moral superiority over those who have. Indeed, I believe if we take habitual drunkards as a class, their heads and their hearts will bear an advantageous comparison with those of any other class.

I have not inquired at what period of time the use of intoxicating liquors commenced; nor is it important to know. It is sufficient that, to all of us who now inhabit the world, the practice of drinking them is just as old as the world itself—that is, we have seen the one just as long as we have seen the other.

Those who have suffered by intemperance personally, and have reformed, are the most powerful and efficient instruments to push [a] reformation to ultimate success. It does not follow that those who have not suffered have no part left them to perform. Whether or not the world would be vastly benefited by a total and final banishment from it of all intoxicating drinks seem to me not now an open question.

. . . There seems ever to have been a proneness in the brilliant and warm-blooded to fall into the vice—the demon of intemperance ever seems to have delighted in sucking the blood of genius and of generosity. What one of us but can call to mind some relative, more promising in youth than all his fellows, who has fallen a sacrifice to his rapacity? He seems ever to have gone forth like the Egyptian angel of death, commissioned to slay, if not the first, the fairest born of every family.

An . . . error, as it seems to me, into which the old reformers fell [prohibitionists of the 1800's], was the position that all habitual drunkards were utterly incorrigible, and therefore must be turned adrift and damned without remedy in order that the grace of temperance might abound, to the temperate then, and to all mankind some hundreds of years thereafter. There is in this attitude something so repugnant to humanity, so uncharitable, so coldblooded and feelingless, that it never . . . can enlist the enthusiasm of a popular cause.

ABRAHAM LINCOLN
February 1862

CHAPTER I

You Don't Have a Disease

" . . . and the inhabitants shall not say, 'I am sick.' " (Isaiah 33:24)

There's good news and better news for all those who are caught up in a compulsive drinking habit which is having an adverse effect on their lives and on the lives of others.

The good news is that ALCOHOLISM IS NOT A DISEASE!

The better news is that IT IS POSSIBLE FOR ANY ALCOHOLIC TO FIND TOTAL AND LASTING RELEASE FROM THE COMPULSION TO DRINK!

There are untold millions who live in despair because they believe they have an illness for which there is no cure. They've been told that once afflicted with alcoholism they'll never find victory over it. They've been told the most they can ever hope for is to stay sober for only one day at a time and to touch one drop of liquor would mean activating the disease in full force again.

Such a philosophy is contrary to what I am

about to tell you. Who am I?

I am your Creator and your God! I'm the one who knows you better than you will ever know yourself. I'm the one who breathed the very breath of life into you. I know how many hairs you have on your head as well as how many drinks you've ever consumed without even bothering to count.

What I'm going to tell you may seem harsh at times, but let me assure you these words are spoken in love and with concern because you need to know what's happening to you. You need to know how to find complete freedom from your bondage.

You see, you have been coddled and counseled and cajoled and pampered and waited on and worried about and confronted by those who beat around the bush long enough. It's time you considered what your God has to say on the subject because I'm the source of all truth. DRUNKENNESS IS AN ABOMINATION TO ME! Please try to comprehend that statement because it's a key to your victory.

Let Me explain that abominations are those acts by which people destroy themselves and others. Engaging in abominations of any sort separates man from God, and when that happens, there is always suffering. Further, the behavior of those who engage in compulsive drinking is such as to be repulsive to others. They, as I, shrink with shuddering from the drunken person because his actions are disgusting.

But I am more than disgusted with your engaging in such destructive activity. I am angered by it and I am grieved. It gives me great sorrow to see you separate yourself from Me as you are, and it grieves the people who love you because they too are hurt by your actions.

When you choose drunkenness as your way of life, you're following Satan who is the prince of darkness and the source of all evil in the world. You're worshipping him as your God. He and his forces are constantly roaming the earth, seeking whom they might devour and you are one of them. He may be encouraging you this very moment to stop reading this book because he knows you will learn the truth about your problem. He knows he could lose his influence on you. He knows I could set you free from his grip on your life, and let Me assure you he doesn't want that. Let Me assure you also that he hates you and nothing would please him more than to have you be totally destroyed by alcohol.

BUT I LOVE YOU! I love you so much I sent My son to die for you. You don't *have* to live the way you do. You don't *have* to be as miserable as you are. You don't *have* to follow Satan.

I created you in My image if you can grasp that thought. You were perfect. Your body is a miracle of creation. You have no right to destroy it.

Please don't tell Me it's your body and that

you can do anything you like with it. It is not your body. It is merely your vehicle to use while you're on earth. It is the tangible form I gave you to house your spirit, mind and soul. It is My temple and My Holy Spirit is to dwell there.

I did not create you with any kind of chemical imbalance. I did not give you a compulsion for alcohol. You do NOT have a disease!

I'm fully aware many alcoholics would like to believe they do because that would absolve them from any guilt they might have for making such a mess of their lives.

I'm also aware you've been told by doctors and psychiatrists, other authorities and friends that you have a disease and that there's no cure for it.

That concept is a lie of the devil—fostered and perpetuated by him to keep you in darkness and in ignorance and to keep you from Me! The fact that many good people believe it does not make it truth.

Of course many would like to believe there is no cure so that they can continue in their insidious habit and say to themselves and others, "Well, I'm sorry but I have to drink because I have this horrible disease. There isn't any cure for it so I'm trapped!"

But think for a moment. If alcoholism were a disease, why haven't your doctors and scientists found a cure for it?

Is it because they're not intelligent? They've been brilliant in discovering cures for other diseases and in developing methods of alleviating the suffering for others. No, it isn't because they lack intelligence.

Is it because they haven't tried?

They've spent billions of dollars and billions of hours trying to find a cure for it. No, it isn't because they haven't tried.

Is it because they don't care? Of course not! There are and have been thousands upon thousands of dedicated men and women who desperately want to find the answer and have been trying to find it for many years.

The reason they cannot or will not find a cure is that THERE IS NO CURE. AND THERE IS NO CURE BECAUSE THERE IS NO DISEASE!

There can be no cure for a disease that doesn't exist.

When I told the people of Israel if they would do certain things they would be afflicted with "none of these diseases," I never mentioned alcoholism. Read the Bible. It is My Word. In Exodus and other Old Testament books, I'm talking about such diseases as leprosy, the Black Death, syphillis, typhoid, cholera and dysentary. I told Moses to tell My people that if they followed certain sanitary procedures (things it took modern medicine centuries to learn) they would prevent the spread of contagious diseases.

And further I said "If thou wilt diligently hearken to the voice of the Lord thy God and will do that which is right in His sight and wilt give ear to His commandments and keep all His statutes, I will put none of these diseases upon thee, which I have brought upon the Egyptians: for I am the Lord that healeth thee!"[1]

No, I didn't mention alcoholism because ALCOHOLISM IS NOT A DISEASE!

Then what is it, you ask? It is a work of the flesh. IT IS A SIN! And sin is of the Devil you serve. It is not of My making.

Again I refer you to My Word. "Now the deeds of the flesh are evident, which are: immorality, impurity, sensuality, idolatry, sorcery . . . DRUNKENNESS . . . and things like these, of which I tell you just as I have told you in times past that those who practice such things shall not inherit the kingdom of God!"[2]

No, alcoholism is not a disease. People don't "practice" diseases. Do you practice cancer? Do you practice influenza before you can catch the flu? Do you practice diabetes before you become ill with it? Do you practice dysentary or malaria or multiple sclerosis or heart disease? No, man does not "practice" disease.

But man does practice sin and when he does

---

1. Exodus 15:26.
2. Galatians 5:19-21.

so, desire takes over and he becomes ensnared because he feels a compulsion to continue in it. And Satan is there at the heart of it. He draws you every step of the way. He is powerful. Is it any wonder that compulsion is so strong?

Do not say you have a disease. Disease is not sin. If it were, there might have been an eleventh commandment which said, "Thou shalt not contract any diseases."

I gave no such commandment because DRUNKENNESS IS A SIN!

Now the following is a partial list of diseases and what causes them:

Germs or bacteria cause such diseases as pneumonia, tetanus, typhoid, scarlet fever, whooping cough and leprosy.

Allergies cause such diseases as asthma, hay fever, hives, conjunctivitis and exzema.

Environmental disorders cause such diseases as sunstroke, frostbite, gangrene, lead poisoning and radiation sickness.

Fungi cause such diseases as thrush, athletes foot, jungle rot and lumpy jaw.

Nutritional deficiencies cause such diseases as beriberi, pellagra, rickets and scurvy.

Parasites cause such diseases as ringworm, malaria, sleeping sickness and trichinosis.

And viruses cause such diseases as chicken pox, measles, mumps, yellow fever and influenza.

No parasite, no fungus, no environmental fac-

tor, no virus, no allergy, and no nutritional
deficiency ever caused alcoholism. It is no
disease!

I have compassion on those who have diseases. Jesus healed the sick and the diseased.
Read the New Testament. You will find Him
healing leprosy. You will find Him healing the
woman who had had an issue of blood for years.
He caused the lame to walk, the deaf to hear and
the blind to see. He had compassion on them and
through My power, He healed them!

Your God does not have any sympathy for
those who willingly engage in drunkenness.

I LOVE THE DRUNKARD, YES, BUT I
DETEST HIS SIN.

Sin is an abomination. Unless you turn from
it, you will be eternally separated from Me along
with Satan because My new heaven and new
earth must be free of all such abominations so
that My saints can live in eternal peace and joy.

I weep for you. My heart grieves for you, but I
can do no other thing for I am a just and righteous God. I have given you the power and the
freedom of choice.

Why are you an alcoholic?

You are an alcoholic because you choose to
drink alcohol to excess and for no other reason!

You choose not to be temperate in all things
as I have commanded you.

Satan himself has you in his power because
you have chosen to serve him and not Me!

No, you don't have a disease so there is no cure.

There is, however, a way of deliverance as there is from all sin.

CHAPTER II

I'm On To Your Games

Whether you're aware of it or not, you're trying to delude Me and My people about your drinking by playing certain games; and let Me assure you I'm aware of every single one. Your loved ones are aware of them too though you believe you're pulling one over on them.

The truth is you're playing the part of a fool; and as fine and as intelligent a person as you truly are, I'm certain you don't want that. Let Me point out some of your games, then, so that you can recognize them for what they are. You may feel inclined to deny them, but please remember that truth is truth whether you deny it or not.

Game 1. HIDE THE BOTTLE.

Recognize that one? Of course you do. You've got one under that easy chair in your living room. You've got one behind that row of books in your book case. There's one under your bed, one under the seat of your car. There's even one in your wood pile. You've got one under the dirty clothes in your hamper. You've got booze in that thermos bottle you're taking to work. (You think because it's Vodka nobody will be able to detect the smell of it on your breath. You're wrong there too.) You've got a bottle on the shelf of your closet, and some of you have even got one buried in your garden! You know exactly just where to dig.

You know where every single bottle is. So do I.

You're drinking to excess and you know it. That's the reason you're hiding your bottles. You say you hide them because your wife is such a prude about drinking. You say it's best not to let the children see you have liquor in your home. You say it's convenient to have the booze where you're working or relaxing so that you don't have to run get it all the time. You say you don't want anybody else drinking your stock. You can't afford to pour one for everybody or anybody who wants one. You say it's good to have a little nip now and then wherever you are. The truth is you're drinking too much and you know it. If you weren't, you wouldn't be trying to hide it. You'd keep your bottle out in the open. You're hiding it because you're ashamed of it. You're ashamed of your drinking. You're ashamed of the amount you consume. You're ashamed of yourself. And somehow you feel if people don't know how much you're drinking, they can't accuse you of imbibing too much.

Truly that's ridiculous, isn't it? People know. They can tell by the way you act. They don't have to know how much you've consumed.

And *I* can tell because I know exactly how much you drink. I also know why you drink. You cannot deceive your Creator.

Game 2. POINT THE FINGER (also known as THE BLAME GAME).

Here you are accusing other people or conditions in your life for making you drink. You are saying, "Well, so I drink too much but there's a reason . . ."

You point the finger at your spouse and say you wouldn't drink if your wife didn't nag or if your husband paid more attention to you.

You point the finger at your parents and say you wouldn't drink if they weren't so hard on you or if they really cared about you.

That's all delusion and you know it. You and you alone are to blame for your drinking. No one else.

You point the finger at your job and say you wouldn't drink if there weren't so many pressures. You say you're a salesman and you're expected to drink with your clients. You say you have to travel all the time and sitting alone nights in motel rooms gets boring. What else is there to do?

Those are delusions and you know it. There is

no job which requires you to be an alcoholic. No salesman is ever expected to be a drunk. You don't become an alcoholic because of traveling. You become an alcoholic by drinking to excess and you know it.

What else is there to do? I can think of many things. Go visit My people in the hospitals, in the nursing homes. Write a letter to a loved one. Read a good book. Go for a walk and rejoice at My creation. Read My Word.

You point the finger at dissatisfaction and say you wouldn't drink if you had a better job or a more understanding mate or whatever.

You point the finger at your town and say you wouldn't drink if you could just move to another place.

You point the finger at loneliness and say you wouldn't drink if you were surrounded by people who cared or who were fun to be with or people you could go places with.

You point the finger at society and say everybody drinks these days. Constantly you see liquor advertised . . . on billboards, in movies, in magazines and newspapers. You say you wouldn't drink if you hadn't been brainwashed into thinking it's the in-thing, the chic-thing, the macho-thing.

You point the finger at an alcoholic parent and say you drink because you inherited the weakness from your mother or your father. Alcoholism is not inherited and you know it.

You point the finger at pain and say you drink to relieve it . . . or at nerves and say it helps to soothe them . . . or at unhappiness and say it helps you to forget your problems.

You and you alone must accept the blame for your actions. There is no one and no condition you can fault for your drinking.

GAME 3. THE GOOD REASON GAME.

You say you drink because alcohol is a stimulant. Everybody needs a stimulant. That's a delusion. Alcohol is a depressant. It deadens certain functions such as judgment, self-criticism and self control and you know it. Your body and mind are depressed by alcohol, not stimulated.

You say you drink because it's cold and alcohol makes you warm. That's a delusion. It may cause the face to flush and the skin to feel warm, but it isn't. Your body is actually losing heat. In severe weather conditions, alcohol consumption would actually increase your chances of dying from the cold.

You say you drink because alcohol makes you feel brave. That's a delusion. You may become more active and excited at first, but you are not brave. Your judgment is poorer and you accomplish less. You make foolish mistakes. You take foolish risks. You are not brave; you are endangering yourself and others. No brave person does that.

You say you drink because alcohol makes you

think more clearly. That's a delusion. Your inhibitions are loosened and you become more talkative. That makes you *think* you are performing better when in reality your thinking processes and reasoning ability are dulled.

You say you drink because alcohol improves your creative ability. That's a delusion. Your creative ability is a God-given ability and I don't need alcohol to bring out the best in you. George Bernard Shaw put it this way: "Alcohol knocks off the last inch of efficiency which in all really fine work makes the difference between first rate and second rate." He's right.

You say you drink because alcohol makes you a better athlete in competition. That's a delusion. You just think you perform better. Actually your reaction time is dulled and to be a good athlete you have to react quickly and with good judgment. Alcohol slows you down, it doesn't speed you up. And if you're hung over, you can't possibly perform with agility and precision.

You say you drink because alcohol improves your digestion. That's a delusion. Alcohol actually increases the flow of acid, thus irritating the lining of your stomach. If you want an ulcer, keep it up.

You say you drink because alcohol improves your eyesight. That's a delusion. Alcohol interferes with the coordination of the eye muscles and can cause double vision. It also interferes

‒ with the interpretation of the images your brain
‒ receives . . . and you may see things that aren't
‒ there . . . or not see things that are. *(or hear)*

You say alcohol is valuable as a sedative or as
a pain killing drug and that's why you drink it.
There are better ways and better drugs which can
‒ be used for either. Things that aren't habit form-
‒ ing and destructive.

You say alcohol can prevent or cure a cold.
That's a delusion. It makes you *feel* warmer and
deadens the reflexes, but it causes the pores to
dilate and therefore makes you more susceptible
to chilling. Also, the drinker's resistance to sickness and disease is lowered, thus he's more likely
to get such complications as pneumonia.

You say alcohol helps you to have a good
time . . . you can't have fun without it. That's a
delusion. You don't know what a really good time
‒ is. You don't have to pay a price for a good time
‒ . . . destroying your body is not necessary for
‒ having fun.

You say alcohol is good for the heart and is
valuable in the treatment of heart disease.
That's a delusion. Nitroglycerine is far more effective than alcohol in relieving the pain of angi-
na. Alcohol has very little beneficial effect in di-
lating blood vessels which supply blood to the
heart muscle.

‒ You say a little alcohol is good for the health.
‒ That's a delusion. There is no scientific evidence

of that if you need scientific evidence.

It cures snake bite? Come on, you know better.

Face it, there are no *good* reasons for drinking. Stop playing that game.

Game 4. THE DARK DRINKS GAME.

You know this one. You're pouring yourself a double or triple shot of booze while you give everybody else a single. That way you can say you've had no more drinks than anybody else has . . . so you don't drink too much. It's all in "their" heads. A delusion.

Game 5. HIDE-THE-SCENT GAME, and HIDE-THE-FACE GAME.

The peppermint candy doesn't hide the fact you've been drinking. The mouthwash doesn't hide it. That gum doesn't hide it. The odor is coming out through your pores. You're sweating it in other words. And that face make-up doesn't hide the small red lines either . . . the puffy face. People know. *I* know.

Game 6. THE I'M-NOT-AN-ALCOHOLIC-BECAUSE GAME . . .

You're a past master at this one. But you're pulling the wool over no one's eyes but your own.

You say you're not an alcoholic because you can quit any time you want to. If you could, you

— wouldn't make such a remark in the first place.

You're not an alcoholic because you can go long periods without drinking . . . you only drink periodically in other words.

You're not an alcoholic because you drink only beer. You don't drink the "hard stuff." Or you drink only wine and wine is good for you. Nonsense. Alcohol is alcohol. And it isn't the amount you drink. It's what happens to you when you drink. *violent, destructive* ←

abusive (language)

You say you're not an alcoholic because you plan to quit tomorrow. You'll quit when you get through this crisis, or when your family gets together again, or after you marry that girl or that man. That's all delusion and you know it.

Game 7. The TIME-YOUR-DRUNKS GAME.

You know this one well. You're taking antabuse because it's been prescribed by your doctor or your psychiatrist. You know that if you drink while it's still in your body you'll become terribly ill. You don't want that, so you plan ahead. You know, for example, that it takes some five days or so for the effects of antabuse to leave your system. So you take your daily pill on Monday, then you omit it on Tuesday, Wednesday, Thursday and Friday so that you can go on a good one Saturday night because that's the night of the big party. Oh, you'll remove those extra pills from the bottle in your medicine chest so that your wife will think you've taken them because you're sure she's counting. But you're not fooling her ... you're not fooling Me. You're only deluding yourself.

And then you get to the point where you're not just sure when those good times might come up ... you want to be prepared ... you don't want to miss out ... so instead of taking a whole pill, you break it in half so in case you happen to drink you'll get only half as sick. But then you get smart. You realize that even being half sick is really pretty bad. You decide to break your pill into quarters so you take only a fourth at a time. Being half as sick as half sick ought to be easier ... so you think ... until you realize that even *that's* more sick than you care to be.

It's a ridiculous game, it's a stupid game. Don't you agree? I gave you better sense than that!

Game 8. THE PERFECT HOST OR HOSTESS GAME.

Don't kid yourself. I know why you're inviting those people into your house. You're going to offer them a drink because it's the hospitable thing to do. The real reason is of course, that *you* want a drink and of course if they're drinking it wouldn't be polite if you didn't. Besides, you know if you're drinking in their presence, your wife or your husband or your children can't say anything about it. They'll have to go along with your scheme. And then you keep offering your guests another and another because *you* want another and another. The more you pour the more hospitable you are, the more generous you are, the more congenial you are. Aren't you the perfect host though? Just look how good you are

— to all those people. That's all delusion.

Game 9. THE YOU-GO-ON-AHEAD GAME and I'VE GOT-TO-RUN-AN-ERRAND GAME.

Now your wife or your husband and your children know that when you send them to the car to wait while you pretend you have to check the lights or the locks or whatever, what you're actually going to do is take a nip. "You go on ahead and I'll be right there" is a ruse that doesn't fool anybody. Neither does that "I've got to run an errand" game. What you're saying is, "I've got to buy some booze even though I *say* I need to pick up some milk at the grocery or a screwdriver at the hardware store. Don't give Me that malarkey. Don't give your family that malarkey either. Everybody knows better.

Game 10. The PICK-A-FIGHT GAME.

I know why you're provoking your mate to

– anger or your children to wrath. It's because
you'll have an excuse to storm out of the house so
you can get drunk. I know why you're berating
your wife for burning the toast or not pressing
your shirts the way you like them or why you're
so upset with your children for not doing well in
school or for making mistakes. I know why you
keep at them and keep at them until they weep.
You can't stand tears you say, so you've got to
have a drink. The way they act, you say, is
enough to drive anybody to drink. How shame-
– ful! I have commanded you not to provoke your
– children to wrath. I have told you to love the wife
– or husband I gave you. I have given you the re-
– sponsibility of caring for them, of seeing to it
– they are protected, that their needs are met
✠ . . . and you are making their lives miserable.

Don't stomp out of the bedroom for a drink
because your partner has refused sex with you
and say your right as a husband or a wife has
been denied. You know the real reason you're doing this and hurting them. You want a drink so
you pretend they're driving you to it. How my
– heart aches for them! What husband or wife
– wants to go to bed with a drunk? How can he or
she be expected to come to you with warmth and
openness when you've got booze on your breath
– and her heart is grieved and breaking? You are
– repulsive to your mate when you're drunk. How
– can you expect it to be otherwise? You repulse
– *Me* when you're drunk.

The sex act is a beautiful thing when there is love involved and I gave that to you as My gift. You have no right to make a mockery of it. I made you to be one flesh . . . I want the two of you to come together as one. You cannot do that when one of you is drunk!

Husbands, I've given your wives the command to be submissive to you, that's true. But your wife is to be submissive when you act like the husband I want you to be. She cannot be submissive to you when you're acting like a crazed animal.

Wives, I've given your husbands this command: "Love your wives and do not be harsh with them."[1]

But you are making it difficult for your husband to love you by being a drunk. You are provoking his harshness by doing things to anger him. You have the responsibility to be a good wife and you cannot accept that responsibility when you are drinking all the time.

Both of you have been given the responsibility to "Train up your children in the way they should go."[2] You are training your children how to drink, how to argue, how to deceive others, how to avoid responsibility: you are training them how to behave as alcoholics.

Children, I've commanded you to honor your

---

1. Colossians 3:19.
2. Proverbs 22:6.

father and your mother. I've placed them in authority over you. You are disobeying Me by disobeying them.

Are you drinking when they have asked you not to? Are you bringing them shame? Are you grieving them with your alcoholism? Are you picking fights with them so you'll have an excuse to hang one on? If you are, you are sinning against Me!

Stop playing the pick-a-fight game. You have no right to drag My people down with you. What's more, you aren't fooling anyone.

Game 11. THE GO-FOR-HELP GAME.

This is perhaps the most deceitful of all and you know it well. So do I. This is the game you play when, after getting too much pressure from your family or your friends or your boss, you promise you'll seek help. The heat is really on so you think you'd better cool that wife down a bit before she leaves you, or that husband before he leaves you, or that boss before he fires you.

You need a little peace and quiet from the pressure anyway so you make an appointment and head for help. The truth is you don't really want help and you don't really intend to accept it. You're just going through the motions so everybody will *think* you are making an effort to quit.

Now when you go to that doctor or that minister or that psychiatrist or that counselor, you're going to try to make that person think you don't really have a problem. The problem is your wife or your husband. They're the ones who need some counseling . . . perhaps marriage counseling would help . . . perhaps family counseling would help. You want everybody around you to see where they're making mistakes. You yourself might drink a little too much, true, but you wouldn't if *they* would settle down or shape up or get off your case or whatever. You're really smart, you're cagey, and you think you are pulling the wool over the eyes of your counselors . . . and maybe you are. But you're deluding yourself; you're not fooling Me.

You'll play this game time and time again. You'll go for help once every six weeks or six months or a year . . . whenever the heat gets unbearable, whenever you're really caught between a rock and a hard place. Then you'll tell your loved ones you aren't getting that much help from so and so; maybe you'll have to try somebody else.

So you try somebody else . . . you change doctors, you change programs, you change psychiatrists, you change ministers. Anything to stall for time. *What a fool you are! How much you're hurting your loved ones!* You give them false hopes and then you dash those hopes again and again until they're sick and weary and afraid. After a time, they don't believe you will ever quit . . . they have no hope, and that's a sad state to be in. They care so much. They love you so much.

So now, you see, you're back to playing the *Blame Game*. You tell your counselors you could quit if you weren't kept from it by your wife or your kids—in other words, that they're not helping you.

You tell your wife or your husband or your children you could quit if only you could get the right kind of counseling because the counselors you have aren't helping you.

Stop expecting others to help you. Stop expecting others to save you. Your wife can't save you, your kids can't save you, your counselors can't save you, your friends can't save you, your ministers can't save you.

You are sinning. You and you alone. No one else can commit your sin for you and no one can save you from it . . . not even yourself.

Only I, your God, can save you from sin. There is no other way.

My child, isn't it time you stopped playing games? They really aren't fun anymore, are they? What good do they do? You're not deceiving anyone. Don't you know that? Let me quote from My Word: "Be not deceived. God is not mocked. For whatsoever a man soweth, that shall he also reap. He that soweth to the flesh shall of

- the flesh reap corruption.[1]

※ Alcoholism is a sin of the flesh and you are
- reaping corruption. You know that. Perhaps
- what you don't know is that "the wages of sin is
- death."[2]

Do you really want to die?
There *is* a way to avoid it.

Don't delude yourself either by saying that you do a good job at work.

That won't save you. Violence, destruction, verbal abuse, alcoholism are all sins against the flesh, & they are all against God's word. These things are all evil & they <u>destroy the soul</u>.

Being an ace at work won't save you, either.

1. Galatians 6:7-8.
2. Romans 6:23.

CHAPTER III

Look What You've Done to My Temple

A temple, as you know, is an edifice which is created for one purpose: that those who enter in, worship and glorify God. Men build temples of wood or stone; and in that sense they are creators because they have taken raw materials and a vision and have constructed buildings which did not exist before in tangible form. They have built many beautiful and glorious temples and the builders take pride in them as do the people who worship there. They have a right to be pleased with their creations. I am pleased.

But only I can create living temples. Know ye not that you are the temple of God? I created that body of yours to dwell in. That is true, but I also created it as an edifice to glorify Me because it is My very best work of creation and I'm proud of it. While you're living in it, you are meant to worship Me from within and without.

When you willfully destroy that temple, as you are with your drinking, you are making that

39

body a pig sty, a hell hole in which to live and move and have your being. Is it any wonder you are miserable living within it? That's because you're using it for a purpose for which it was never intended.

To give you an analogy, you are tearing down the walls, you are piling up debris, you are destroying the heating system, the electrical system, the plumbing system, you're breaking the windows, you're wrecking the furnishings . . . in general, you're making the place of your dwelling a shambles. As a result, you not only find it uncomfortable to live there, but soon you won't be able to. You'll be forced to abandon it; and once you do, there is only one place to go . . . through death's door.

I've given you two alternatives: one, you can choose to be with Me in heaven where there's eternal joy, health, peace and creative work to perform, or you can choose the sort of hell you know now. But let Me warn you, that existence will be far worse than you can envision it because I won't be there to lessen the full onslaught of sin and suffering. As it is now, My Spirit is in the world and you are reaping the benefits of that even though you are choosing destruction.

You are free to love My creation and rejoice in its beauty now. You are free to love My people and to know the warmth of their friendship now.

The house you dwell in is a clear reflection of your spiritual state.

There are people here to help you, to serve you, even to take care of you now. There won't be then.

All the good which you know in this life will be removed once you pass through death's door without Me. All the sickness, suffering, and sin and ugliness and devastation you now see in the world and feel in your body will be yours for eternity unless you choose otherwise.

Let Me give you some idea just what a magnificent structure it is you're tearing apart.

Consider the brain. No creation of Mine is a more astounding, a more miraculous structure than that. Let Me quote My servant Og Mandino in his book *The Greatest Miracle in the World:*

> Your brain is the most complex structure in the universe . . . Within its three pounds are thirteen billion nerve cells, more than three times as many cells as there are people on earth. To help you file away every perception, every sound, every taste, every smell, every action you have experienced since the day of your birth, I have implanted, within your cells, more than one thousand billion billion protein molecules. Every incident in your life is there waiting only your recall. And, to assist your brain in the control of your body I have dispersed, throughout your form, four million pain-sensitive structures, five hundred thousand touch detectors, and more than two hundred temperature detectors. No

nation's gold is better protected than you. None of your ancient wonders are greater than you. You are my finest creation.*

And what are you doing with that brain? You are poisoning it! Make no mistake about it, alcohol is as much a poison as is arsenic or strychnine. The leading doctors in your world will tell you that. Dr. Charles Mayo for an example.

Where does this particular poison go once you ingest it? To the brain! You are poisoning My most miraculous structure!

What is happening to your brain as a result of that poison? It is shrinking for one thing. If you had had X-rays taken of it before you began drinking and were to take them now, you would see the extent to which it has shrunk and you would be frightened.

Your nerve cells are deteriorating as a result of that poison and the results of that are loss in judgment, intellectual capacity and moral power or conscience. It is the cortex, the higher part of your brain, which is affected first, and that is the area in which your thoughts are initiated. You are poisoning your reason, your will, your entire character.

The day will come, if it hasn't already, that

---

*Reprinted by permission of Frederick Fell Publishers, Inc., 386 Park Avenue South, New York, NY 10016, from the book, *The Greatest Miracle in the World* ($5.95) by Og Mandino, copyright 1975 by Og Mandino.

you will no longer be able to reason or to think or to remember. Your intellectual interests will wane until you have nothing left but the awful, insatiable craving for another drink. You won't be able to perceive things clearly, to judge correctly or even to make a decision. It takes nerve energy to do those things and you are poisoning those cells, depriving them of the good nutrition they require to produce that energy.

And finally, you will no longer be able to tell right from wrong. You won't know the difference between truth and falsehood, between reality and fantasy, between brutality and gentleness. You will lie, you will be brutal, you will be pathetic if you aren't already. You will be filled with arrogance and egotism, and no one will want to be around you. You will be loathsome to others. Is it any wonder you are an abomination to Me?

You are also poisoning the sensory control area of your brain. From this area your emotions, your senses, your motion or motor ability and your sex instincts are controlled. But you are interfering with these functions.

You are prone to accident, you drop things. You stagger, you weave, you fall. Your senses of touch and taste, of smell, hearing and sight are dulled. You have blurred or double vision, narrowed or tunnel vision, your range of sight is shortened. You find it difficult to distinguish one color from another. Is it any wonder you are a menace on the highways? Is it any wonder there are laws to keep you from driving?

Your emotions are out of control and you overreact to normal irritations. You blow things out of proportion. Is it any wonder those in your household find it nearly impossible to live with you? You act as if you're insane. Eventually you will be incapable of sanity. You will suffer delerium tremens, you will hallucinate. You are becoming a mental case . . . all those things you experience periodically now will soon be yours permanently!

And still you drink.

Your base instincts emerge. You have grotesque desires in sex which you cannot satisfy because your ability to perform at all is slowly being destroyed. You will eventually lose all such desire and you will be rejected by that man or woman whose body you were given to share for the joy of it.

And further, you are destroying that area of your brain which controls your organic functions: circulation, digestion and respiration. If you ingest enough poison to completely affect this area, you will die on the spot!

Meanwhile, those functions are being impaired and the organs which perform those tasks necessary for their functioning are being destroyed.

Take the liver for example. It is the most amazing, the most versatile chemical laboratory in the world. If that liver were to stop functioning you would die within the day!

In that organ, I free the blood of its waste matter and poisons. Your liver is the only organ in your body which can oxidize your alcohol. It can do so only at approximately half an ounce per hour, and that is well in excess of what the normal body would ever need. But you, with your incessant intake of poison, are consuming seven or eight times that amount per hour . . . or more . . . and so that waste is building up and up and up. The day may come when you will die from toxic poisoning. Are you aware of that?

Your liver is also a storehouse of vitamins, minerals and proteins. You need B_{12} for the normal production of red blood cells and to prevent pernicious anemia. Alcohol destroys that vitamin.

Your liver stores iron needed to produce hemoglobin, the red pigment of your blood.

It makes many needed blood proteins, chiefly albumin which decreases the ability of your blood to flow through capillary walls thus preventing edema; fibrinogen which makes the blood clot (or you would bleed to death from a cut); and globulin which provides resistance to disease. Is it any wonder you are so disease prone? That you can scarcely fight off a simple cold?

Your liver manufactures bile which aids in digestion; it removes bodily poison and forms urea which is eliminated with other waste materials in the urine.

Alcohol is irritating that liver and can cause chirrosis, which is a serious disease. In this condition the tissue first thickens because the unhealthy growth of scar tissue is taking place. So your liver is getting larger . . . can you feel it? Later it will shrink because the cells are wasting away. This once healthy, dark red organ will then turn yellow. Once soft and flexible, it will become hard and gritty and lumpy.

If you are drinking to excess you are in serious danger of your life!

And look what you're doing to your heart, the most ingenious pump in the universe! It has to be, for it must pump more than six hundred thousand gallons of life's blood through more than sixty thousand miles of your veins and arteries every year!

That heart beats with a rhythm that's in tune with My very universe! It pulsates some 70 or 80 times every minute of every day, day in and day out, year in and year out . . . as long as you draw breath on this earth!

And you are poisoning the pump! The condition of your heart under alcohol is similar to that which occurs in fatigue in that your pump has to dilate more than it normally would when performing the same amount of work. When the chambers of your heart enlarge abnormally like that, the valves eventually cannot close tight enough to prevent the return of the blood that should be forced onward with each beat. This naturally interferes with your circulation which in turn affects every part of your body. The kidneys, for example. These comprise the most amazing filtering system ever known. Nothing man has devised can equal it. Nothing he will ever devise will surpass it. Your kidneys filter all waste from every drop of blood by use of some million minute coiled tubes through which your blood passes. Waste materials are then sent on to the bladder from which they are eliminated.

You cannot live without this filtering system and you are tearing it down. I fear for you!

You are destroying your stomach. You may have severe gastritis now, but that is just the beginning. Some of you have had a good portion of that stomach removed already. What needless suffering you've inflicted upon yourselves!

But, you say, it takes years and years to destroy yourself so why not live it up for a time yet . . . why not enjoy your maddening cup for just a bit longer . . . there will be time to quit.

You are wrong! The minute alcohol enters your bloodstream, as it does upon entering your body because it doesn't need to be digested, it begins to poison you immediately!

How long you can continue the onslaught is not for you to say. Only I know the day and the hour you will die. Let Me assure you, I did not choose this sort of death for you. You are choosing it. Because I know the time and the hour does not mean I have planned it this way.

For some of you, this very night your soul will be required of you.

Some of you will read these words and die tomorrow. Tomorrow you will stand before Me and give an account of what you have done with your life, of how you have used My temple.

Some of you, you know not whom but I know . . . have only one more week on My earth. Look at the clock. In seven days at this very hour, you will stand before Me, trembling, sober, in shame.

Some of you have but a few more months . . . some a year at the most. Some of you may go on for yet a good number of years and you will beg to die. All of you are wasting the precious time I have given you. All of you are missing out on the glorious life I have in store for you. All of you are tearing down My temple.

Why are you destroying My masterpiece? Your body performs miracles without your bidding. It can perform even greater miracles at your command and with My assistance. Your potential is without limit because I have created you in My image. Why don't you make good use of your temple before it's too late? Why don't you create masterpieces in love, in inspiration? You have that ability. Why don't you begin now before you lose all capacity to think . . . before you lose all control of your bodily functions?

You are the greatest miracle of My creation. You are the greatest temple ever built or that ever will be built. That temple is holy. I created it in My image as I told you, and I am holy. I am your God!

My request that you take care of your body is a reasonable one, is it not? I make no unreasonable demands of My people. I don't ask the impossible of anyone. My command is simply that ". . . you present your bodies a living sacrifice, holy, acceptable unto God, which is your reasonable service." [1]

I'm not asking you to *die*. I gave you *life* and I want that life to be an abundant one for you. Of *course* that precludes taking care of the body you live in!

Look what you've done to My temple! Heed My voice. You are accountable. "Know ye not that ye are the temple of God and that the Spirit of God dwelleth in you? If any man defile the temple of God, him will God destroy; for the temple of God is holy, which temple ye are." [2]

I love you. My heart grieves for you. Won't you put this abomination apart from your life from this moment on?

You can, you know. I will help you. I will save you from sin and destruction.

---

1. Romans 12:1.
2. I Corinthians 3:16-17.

CHAPTER IV

Look What You've Done to My People

You have been told, as have your loved ones, that unless you want to stop drinking for your sake, any attempts to get you to do so will fail. "You *can't* stop until you care enough about yourself to initiate action," you've heard people say. "Stopping for anybody else's sake is not a good enough reason."

But *I* say that concept is based on an untruth originated by the father of lies. No delusion is more cunningly contrived than that one. None is more devious.

Can you name one doctor, one psychiatrist, one counselor, one friend, even one fellow alcoholic who does not believe it? Can you name *anybody* at all?

You see what a thorough job of brainwashing Satan has done by instilling that belief in the minds of men and women everywhere? None is more effective in keeping you from doing what you know you should . . . from doing what you know you must.

Satan knows if he can get you to swallow that one, you won't want to stop until you're in so deep you won't be able to.

He knows if he can get the people close to you believing that, they won't confront you about stopping until it's too late . . . or until the chances are very slim that you will.

He knows that if he can get professionals in the field to believe that, they'll recommend a hands off policy on you until you're beyond the point of no return.

If he can get your children to turn against you, if he can get your mate to leave you, if he can break up your home, if he can get that boss to fire you, if he can keep you drinking until your health breaks, then chances are you'll be too far gone to raise a hand in protest.

Look what you've done to My people!

They crowd the mental institutions, their minds broken from the strain of living with you.

They fill the hospitals, their bodies racked with pain from injuries received in the accidents you have caused and from the blows you have struck them in anger.

They cower in their homes, weeping, distraught and afraid. Their hearts break from the sorrows you have brought them, and the only hope anyone can give them is that you won't stop until you want to.

They go about their work with the heavy burden of a grief that will not be lifted.

They go homeless and hungry because you have wasted the monies intended for their support.

Your children become bitter, then rebellious, and engage in behavior and activities which further the destruction of My people.

And the bodies of those victims who lie in the graveyards could not be counted by any man or woman living on earth. If you were given the actual figure of the number of deaths you have caused, you wouldn't believe it. You couldn't believe it.

It's time you realized you *should* stop drinking for the sake of My people.

If you seek to save your life for your sake, you will lose it.

If you seek to lose your life for My sake, you will find it and in so doing, you will help lift a grief from the world.

You must stop drinking for your sake or your attempts to do so will fail? Don't harbor that delusion any longer! The truth is you should stop for the sake of your wife.

You should stop for the sake of your husband.

You should stop for the sake of your children.

You should stop for the sake of your parents.

You should stop for the sake of anyone who has to deal with you in any way whatsoever.

"There is none righteous, no not one";[1] but no

---

1. Romans 3:10.

matter what wrongs men have done, not one person deserves the kind of treatment you have meted out.

Can you imagine what it would be like to be treated by others the way you have treated them? You couldn't bear it.

I have commanded you, in what man refers to as the Golden Rule, that " . . . all things whatsoever ye would that men should do to you, do ye even so to them," [1] yet you continue your abuse against others as though it makes no difference *how* atrocious your acts against them are.

The deeds of those who committed atrocities against prisoners of any war in history are no more heinous than those you commit against My people . . . nor are they anywhere near so great in number.

No matter how remote the alcohol-related problems of others may seem to you, I want you to know I care about each individual involved; and one person's distress alone is reason enough for you to stop drinking.

A child cried himself to sleep last night because you struck him when he asked you to treat his mother better. In angry words you said, "Stay out of it; this doesn't concern you."

It did concern him of course. The blow you dealt him hurts, both physically and mentally.

---

1. Matthew 7:12.

In his small body he has paid a price because of your actions . . . he has suffered because of you. That boy alone is reason enough that you stop drinking.

A woman is afraid today. She wonders what's going to happen now that you've lost your job because of drinking. She's been looking for work but has no skills for the kind which would pay enough for your family to live on. Then too, there'll be the added expense of a baby sitter since you can't be trusted to care for those children. What shame . . . that you've let it come to this!

I'm saddened that you've forced this concern upon her. I placed *you* as head of your household and you are abdicating that position. Further, you have been a poor manager of the monies I've placed in your hands; and since "it is required in stewards that a man be found faithful," [1] your family is suffering needlessly.

This woman is reason enough for you to stop drinking.

There's a daughter who needs to talk to her mother, but she's forced to go to the mother of a friend. She wishes it could be you, but you're in a world of your own. She doesn't think you care about her . . . you're always drinking. Then too, she wonders what you could tell her anyway. You

---

1. I Corinthians 4:2.

can't cope with your own life, how could you possibly help her with hers?

A small matter you say? That girl is reason enough for stopping.

There's a son who's disappointed because you got to "drinking with the boys" and forgot about your promise to take him somewhere special. That boy's disappointment is reason enough for you to stop.

There's a young girl looking for companionship because she's lonely, and she believes she might find someone in a bar because you've taught her that's the place to go. How sad you've trained her thus! She is reason enough for you to stop drinking.

An innocent father died yesterday. He had pulled his car to the side of the road to fix a tire. Your vision was blurred by alcohol . . . you were driving much too fast. You struck him down and kept on going. You had no idea what you'd hit, but you wondered whether or not it might have been a human being. You and your carload of friends laughed and drove on.

That man's skull was split . . . his chest was crushed. He died calling out the names of his wife and four beautiful children. They'll have to grow up without him now. His grief-struck widow feels dead inside. She wonders what she'll do.

Life is such a precious thing and you've taken it away from this fine man as well as from countless others. You had no right. It was such a needless crime, a senseless crime, a cruel crime.

Don't say I could have prevented it. Preventing it was *your* responsibility. You were given a choice as to how to spend your life.

That man's grieving family is reason enough for you to quit your maddening habit.

A woman committed suicide not long ago. She saw no way out from the misery you inflicted upon her. You were never sober. You berated her, you abused her, you humiliated her, you threatened to kill her if she left you.

Her heart's desire was to be a good wife to you, but you never gave her that chance though you promised to when you married her. You made that vow to her before Me. Do you remember?

Her death alone is reason enough for you to stop drinking.

There's a young woman who's spending her life in a wheel chair because of you. You were driving on the wrong side of the road and struck her car head on. She had to give up all her dreams and hopes and plans. She's had a struggle. She faces life bravely . . . or so it seems to others . . . but I hear her crying in the night and I grieve.

She is reason enough.

There's a husband anxious about you today. He knows when the children come home from school, they'll find you drunk and he's concerned for their well being. His concern alone is reason enough for you to stop.

There's a police officer who's risking his life this very moment as he attempts to stop a quarrel between a drunken man and woman.

He is reason enough.

My people are paying the costs of your destruction and they are angry. I don't blame them. They pay for the care of families you send to welfare because you won't support them. They pay for the public defenders who patrol the streets and highways and endanger their lives to keep you off the roads. They pay for the medical care you require when you're hospitalized without means and for others you hospitalize. They pay for homes to rehabilitate you, for prisons to hold you and even for graves to bury you.

They've spent billions of dollars in research trying to figure out just why you drink and what can be done to stop you.

There is no way for mankind to assess the damage you've done to My people. The files bulge with statistics but they tell only an infinitesimal part of the story. There are crimes and hurts and accidents and injuries and disappointments and waste and broken lives and hearts and homes that no man knows about.

But *I* know, and you shall give an account of every single incident in which you've hurt someone because of your drinking.

You'll give an account of every responsibility you ever walked out on.

You'll give an account of every task you failed to perform, every job you neglected, every dollar you wasted, every unkind word you spoke, every spirit you dragged down, every person you wounded. You'll account for every crime you committed against My people, and not one whit shall you withhold. You will remember it all.

A price must be paid for those sins.

If you choose to repent of them, "I will save you for My name's sake," [1] and "I will lead you in the paths of righteousness for My name's sake." [2]

Should you stop drinking for *your* sake? Isn't it clear you cannot? Deep in your heart you know that . . . you've always known that.

Deep in your heart you know you're unworthy. That's why so many of you say you must improve yourselves before you come to Me. You'll clean up your act first and *then* you'll come, you say.

Satan is delighted to warp your thinking in such a manner. It's a good way for him to buy more time so that he can step up his attacks to destroy you. Don't fall prey to that thinking.

Consider the magnet. There's a positive and a negative side and opposites attract as you know. If you try to put your "good" side toward Me, your "cleaned-up" side, your "improved" side, I

---

1. Psalm 106:8.
2. Psalm 23:3.

can give you no power whatsoever. But if you turn your sinful side to Me, I will draw you unto Myself and give you the power to live a new life.

You cannot lift up your good works before Me and expect to receive deliverance. You must give Me your sins . . . you must repent of them . . . and *then* you will know what it means to be free!

The price for those sins has already been paid by the Lord Jesus Christ. Salvation is My gift to you because I love you, and it's free for the asking.

Isn't it time you stopped drinking? Isn't it time you claimed your deliverance?

Or are you laboring under still other delusions?

CHAPTER V

Examine Your Misconceptions

Perhaps Satan has deluded you into believing certain fallacies other than the disease theory. If so, I would examine these so-called "truths" carefully because you cannot find salvation in untruths. These misconceptions are many and they did not originate with Me. You are being deceived by them and thus kept from taking a hold on your problem and doing something about it. This is exactly what he hopes for.

One misconception you may have fallen prey to is this: you don't actually believe you're an alcoholic because you don't fit the descriptions you've read about alcoholics. I'm not concerned with terminology. Just exactly at which point you cross over from what your man-made descriptions refer to as *heavy drinker* to actual *alcoholic* is not the issue. The criterion you can use is this: does drinking have an adverse effect on your life and/or on the lives of others? If it does, you can bet sin is at the heart of it. It's as simple as that.

Once sin gains a foothold, it begins its insidious task of destroying you and you will feel a compulsion to indulge in it. Eventually you will come to believe it's the compulsion which is at the heart of your problem. That's not true. Compulsion is the result of your "practicing" the sin. Satan is there at the heart of it. He urges you to take another drink and another. He makes you believe it's enjoyable; and then when you're in his grip and cannot break away, he tells you that you have a disease and that no one knows why only one in twelve or one in ten or one in eight will be so affected. It's unfortunate you happen to be that one, he says. You are a victim of circumstance. It really isn't your fault. So he tells you.

So please don't say you don't need help because you don't fit the descriptions. Don't argue that alcoholics black out and since you don't, you're not an alcoholic. Don't argue that alcoholics hide bottles and since you don't, you're not one of them. Don't say that because you can stop after so many drinks that you aren't an alcoholic because an alcoholic can't stop. You'll get to that place yourself, so don't take refuge in that delusion.

Does drinking have an adverse effect on your life and/or on the lives of others? That is the question and you know the answer to it. Has your family brought the subject up? Listen to them. They aren't just voicing their opinions. They are voicing Mine. I am using them for your consul. If anyone is concerned by your drinking and expresses that concern, it could be that I am speaking to you through them. Do not dismiss their comments lightly. Whether these people are born of My Spirit or not, I can and do use them as agents in bringing My message to you.

Terminology is not the issue. It doesn't matter whether the world calls you a serious drinker, a problem drinker, a booze hound, a jug head, a periodic drinker, a drunk, a lush, a sot, a wino or an alcoholic. Don't defend your position by saying you don't fit the description. You fit *My* description as a sinner and that's what really matters.

Another misconception you've been voluntarily victimized by is that you have to hit bottom either physically, mentally or emotionally (or all three) before you can begin the upward climb to sobriety. That is a terrible lie, very artfully contrived by the very sly and cunning devil himself. What a sad thing to believe!

You do *not* have to hit bottom. I will deliver at any moment you call out to Me.

Let me give you an analogy. When you step inside an elevator to go, say to the seventh floor, you do not first have to head for the basement.

You can start going up at exactly the point from which you enter that elevator. If you board a bus in Chicago and the ultimate destination is San Francisco, you don't *have* to go all the way to San Francisco. You can get off at any point along the way. So it is with drinking.

I don't want you to go down into the gutter . . . I don't want you to lose your self-respect, your reputation, your wife or your husband, your family, your home before you begin your upward climb. You don't have to. You can get off that bus now!

Please heed the warning signals. You are in danger. Do *not* proceed with caution. Call upon Me. Turn around. Head the other way!

Here is yet another misconception. You've been told you can't become an alcoholic in a vacuum . . . that it takes other people in order for you to develop such a compulsion. You're told you have to have a "provoker," a "rescuer," a "responder" or whatever. These people do play a part in your game but not because they want to or plan to. You force them into the game by using their love as your wedge.

The truth is, you can become a compulsive drinker wherever you are. You can live alone with no one to speak to, no one to see you, no one to react to your drinking. But you can still be led by Satan into compulsion, captivity and death. Though no one sees, I see. Though no one responds, I respond. You grieve Me because you're suffering.

Yet another misconception is this: once you're an alcoholic, you'll always be an alcoholic. That isn't true. Once you have called to Me for deliverance you are free. You are made whole in My eyes, and that is better than if you had never sinned. I don't continue to see you as a sinner; I see you as redeemed. The grip of compulsion can then be broken. The chains which bind you can snap.

But it will take your cooperation. I can bring you victory only if you live in Me. If you continue in sin, you will continue reaping the rewards of it.

You don't have a disease, remember, so you can't be cured. But you can be set free!

Once freed, can you ever drink again? Why would you ask such a question? If you had a disease the answer could possibly be yes because there are diseases which, once you've had them, give you lasting immunity. There are others against which you can be innoculated and thus you are immune to them. There are diseases which can be cured with proper medical care . . . still others which can be avoided by use of preventive measures. If you knew you'd get a severe rash by walking through a bed of poison ivy, would you willingly walk through it? If you knew you'd get dysentary from drinking contaminated water, would you willingly drink it? Of course not!

If you know what alcohol does to you and you've been delivered from it, why would you want to take another drink?

Another misconception is this: you can't quit drinking because you lack the will power to do so. Don't put yourself in such a category. If you think you lack will power, you're not considering the marvelous way you were made. I created you with will power. I gave it to you so that you could choose the good things in life and thus be able to enjoy and appreciate them. What joy would you experience if you automatically received everything that was good, if you had no choices to make? What would you learn? What would you do? What challenge would there be? I gave you the world over which to have dominion, but that dominion comes to those who choose to have dominion. If you did not choose to service your automobile, would it perform for you? If you did not choose to empty the garbage, would it disappear from your sight?

And what glory would there be to Me if you were forced to love Me? What joy would you know in that kind of love? What freedom? Do your children love you because they choose to or because you command them to? You know the answer. You cannot demand love from anyone.

No, I have given each of you will power and I will not violate your freedom of choice. You are free to choose how you will use that power, but I will not use it for you. You have that freedom and it is a gift. You have an abundance of will power. If you don't believe it, look at what you've accomplished with that power when it comes to the ills in your life. You have reaped many rewards by the "grace" of Satan if you will.

But when you choose rightly, I will help you to reap rewards that will bring you joy, love, peace, freedom. And if you lack the strength to use your will power rightly, you can call upon Me and I will supply it for I am the source of all strength.

Choose you this day whom you will serve.

Satan is strong. I am stronger. Sin is death. I am life. I have overcome Satan and I have overcome death. I have overcome the world. By My grace, you can do likewise.

Yet another misconception is this: you've been told a person's real character emerges when he's under the influence of alcohol; therefore, what you express while drinking is truth and your loved ones and counselors should take note of it. So you believe. But the ugliness you spew forth when your mind is clouded by alcohol is not truth by any stretch of the imagination I gave you.

You buy drinks for others or give away money you can't afford because your real character is emerging you say. You are in reality a very generous person. So you believe. No, My friend. You are not overwhelmed with generosity. You're taking leave of your senses.

Every person has unlimited potential to develop either good and/or bad qualities, but the good cannot emerge when you're under the influence. Your word cannot be relied upon. You cannot be trusted to act wisely. You cannot make accurate judgments.

You are amusing when drunk because you're really a very humorous person. You like to bring laughter to the world. So you believe. No, My friend, your humor is not real. It's pathetic. A true sense of humor is a gift of God. It cannot emerge when you're drunk.

Your real character is not emerging at all. You are Satan's channel when you're drinking, and nothing that is true or right or good can come forth.

I am truth. Satan is the father of lies. I don't express Myself through drunken words and drunken acts. The reality of the character which emerges when you're drinking is sinful.

Another misconception is this: once you get to the point where you truly are in misery, you will be told you are no good to anyone, that you are worthless, that you're a bum.

That is a lie perpetuated by Satan to blind you to the truth of your worth, to the potential that lies within you.

You are more precious to Me than jewels. You are an individual, unique, separate, distinct. I have never created another just like you . . . there is only you. You are an original, a master-piece. You are not diminished because you're you. You're diminished because of sin. It grieves Me to see the suffering you're inflicting upon yourself and others by choosing evil over good, wrong over right and sin over salvation.

Haven't you suffered when you've seen your loved ones doing wrong? Haven't you hurt for them? Haven't you wished you could take their hurts away . . . their hard lessons . . . their pain? You can't and so you grieve.

Please recognize the fact that there is a dignity about you . . . or that there could be. Please know I am proud of you as My creation but that I am saddened by the choices you have made.

Now, the last misconception to which Satan will lead you is this: you will want to consider suicide as your only answer. "Why don't you go ahead and kill yourself?" he'll whisper to you. "You don't have to live like this. You can't go on any longer. Why don't you just put an end to it? If you put a bullet through your brain, your miseries will be over."

Many of you are thinking this right now. You're at the point where you believe there is no alternative but death. You're wrong on two counts:

One, there *is* an alternative.

Two, death will not end your suffering.

That suicide is your only way out is a lie of the devil. Once you die you will be his forever. That's what he's after.

I implore you in love, don't believe his lies. Don't you realize he's in control of your life?

There are no answers in suicide. You must

come to Me before you pass through death's door, and " . . . he that cometh to Me I will in no wise cast out."[1] At this time you may be rejected by everyone you've ever known on earth, but I will not turn away from you. I will hear you. I will deliver you.

And please know this also: you have no more right to take your life than you have to take the life of another. Remember what I said to you in the beginning . . . that body is yours to use, but it is *My* temple. Only I have the authority to say when you shall put it aside. I have not given you that authority. "It is appointed unto men once to die . . . "[2] and *I* am to make that appointment. Not you.

I am longsuffering. I am not willing that any should perish. If you are going on when you think you can go on no longer, perhaps it is because I will not let you go.

I am holding onto your hand while you're being swept under the raging current because I don't want you to die!

Please don't take matters into your own hands and let go. Don't be deluded by Satan's lies. You are the only one of a kind. There is no one who can take your place, and I have glorious

---

1. John 6:37.
2. Hebrews 9:27.

plans for your life. You are My child. I love you. Believe that.

I will save you from sin. I will lead you through the dark waters. I will restore your soul.

CHAPTER VI

I Am Aware How You Feel

No man can practice sin without paying a price because "the wages of sin is death."[1] Sometimes death comes rapidly, sometimes slowly; but because you are drinking, you are deteriorating in mind and body and that will lead to physical death. There is no escaping it. There is yet another death, a spiritual death, and that is far worse than the first. There *is* a way of escape from that, however, for "the gift of God is eternal life through Jesus Christ our Lord."[2]

I know how you feel in your body and the feeling isn't pleasant whether you're suffering from the mild discomfort of a hangover or the excruciating pains of chirrosis.

All of you can describe the hangover. There's the upset stomach, the fatigue, the headache and that awful thirst.

You see, alcohol causes the fluid inside your

1. Romans 6:23.
2. *Ibid.*

73

cells to move outside those cells, thus you have a cellular dehydration even though your total body fluid has not changed appreciably. Therefore your thirst is very real and very great. Water cannot quench it.

And that indigestion is the result of irritation to your stomach. Alcohol is a powerful gastric irritant and the lining of that stomach is severely inflamed. Eating becomes uncomfortable. Food makes you nauseous. Some of you have the extreme pain of an ulcer, some have developed gastric cancer. The pain is unbearable. I am aware.

You would like to vomit from the nausea you feel but you cannot. Perhaps you didn't know that I have placed within your body a precaution against the accidental and rapid ingestion of poison, and that is the vomiting reflex. If poison reaches even 0.12% of your blood level rapidly, that vomiting reflex is activated for your protection. But when you drink steadily, you depress that vomiting center and thus you can consume lethal amounts of poison so long as you remain conscious. Thus, while you may be nauseous, you cannot vomit the poison your body wants to reject. You have turned your body wisdom into body foolishness. It's no wonder you experience such discomfort.

And then there is that headache. Yours may be caused by an allergic reaction to cogeners, the products of the fermentation process which took place when the alcohol was made. Some of those cogeners are extremely toxic and it is no wonder you have a headache which aspirin will not seem to alleviate.

Some of your headaches may be the result of the fatigue you experience because of a low blood sugar level. When you ingest alcohol, your blood sugar increases sharply, but then it drops sharply and that resultant low blood sugar level can cause the kind of headache and fatigue which lasts for many hours. Those feelings are very real and will never leave you completely unless you stop drinking.

And you feel warm, do you not? The reason for this is that the alcohol has dilated your peripheral blood vessels, bringing much of your life's blood to the outer surfaces. The feeling is distressful. But while you may feel warm, you are actually losing your body heat and are subject to chilling and subsequent colds and pneumonia. I know what discomfort those problems bring you.

If you're drinking regularly to excess, you never feel good, do you? You've forgotten what it is to feel good. Don't you sometimes long for that feeling?

And you've experienced the extreme discomfort of a jittery, burning sensation that will not go away no matter what you do, haven't you? You feel as though you are wound up so tight you will spring apart into millions of fragments given the slightest impetus. You're feeling this way for a reason. The cells of your nervous system operate as telephone wires carrying messages day and night . . . through your brain and to all parts of your body. The axones (string-like elongations of nerve cells—sometimes several feet long) are affected because the alcohol "burns" along these lines. You are jittery, you are jumpy; that burning sensation is very, very real.

You know that alcohol burns when you place a fire to it. That's where the term *proof* originated. When alcohol was poured over gun powder, that powder would ignite if the alcohol content were at approximately 50%. In other words, when the gun powder exploded and burned, you had proof of the alcohol content of the liquid. You realize, don't you, that some of the alcohol you drink is dangerously near the explosive level? Is it any wonder you experience that burning sensation? It's proof of the poison in your body, you can be sure of that.

Not infrequently, those axones or nerve cells become inflated because of lack of proper nourishment, and thus you experience a painful condition known as neuritis. You can scarcely lift your hands to wash your face or comb your hair. That pain is very real. I understand your suffering.

Some of you have developed partial paralysis of certain muscles because cells have atrophied as a result of the poison. This is giving you much frustration and anxiety. I don't blame you for those feelings. You have reason to be upset and afraid.

Some of you are experiencing pain because of built up pressure in your veins. The pain is acute. You see, your liver may be hardening and when the blood cannot flow freely through it, the pressure must build. Thus it could be that your lower extremities are badly swollen, making you terribly uncomfortable. Your stomach may be so swollen or distended with fluid you can scarcely breathe. It's an awful feeling. Some of you have had, or will have to have, that acute distress relieved by having a doctor insert a hollow tube through the wall of that huge stomach so that the fluid can be drained from your body. That fluid will keep building up, sad to say, and at shorter and shorter intervals, so you truly do have a serious and most painful problem.

And some of you, again because of pressure build-up, are finding a ballooning of the veins in your esophagus. It's painful to swallow, isn't it? It's also dangerous because those thinned-out veins are likely to rupture and can cause serious or fatal hemorrhage.

Yes, your physical distress is very real. Your suffering is beyond description. But then, you can expect it to be. You're poisoning yourself. Surely you couldn't expect to feel good when you're drinking poison every day. You're dying, and death by poison is excruciating.

And I know the pain of withdrawal when you try to stop drinking. Those awful tremors just won't go away unless you have another drink. Those convulsions . . . they too are terrible. And the hallucinations—some of you know how awful they can be. You can't help being terribly frightened because they are indeed very frightening.

The severity of delirium tremens cannot be measured. Some of you have experienced them. Truly they are unbearable because they totally and completely terrorize you. Is it any wonder that many have died in the throes of such delirium? Is it any wonder so many have become insane?

You think I am unaware of how you feel? I have told you these things in My Word. I warned you against the folly of drinking.

"Listen, My son and be wise, be guided by good sense: never sit down with tipsy men or among gluttons; the drunkard and the glutton come to poverty, and revelling leaves men in rags . . . Who shriek? Who groan? Who quarrel and grumble? Who are bruised for nothing? Who have bleary eyes? Those who linger over the bottle, those who relish blended wines. Then look not on the wine so red, that sparkles in the cup; it glides down smoothly at first, but in the end it bites like any snake, it stings you like an adder.

You will be seeing odd things, you will be saying queer things; you will be like a man asleep at sea, asleep in the midst of a storm."[1]

Where is that man or that woman I created in My image? The real you is asleep in that awful storm . . . you no longer know who you really are.

But the distress you feel in your body is nothing compared to the distress you feel in your mind and heart. Am I not correct? You are full of deep remorse and deeper resentments. The deeper the guilt you feel for the way you are living, the deeper your resentments grow for you are desperately trying to justify your behavior. You desperately look for a cross on which to nail your sins so you look to those around you and nourish grievances against them.

These grievances grow and grow like evil weeds until they would choke the very life from you. Memories from your past cross your mind like evil apparitions from the very pit of hell, haunting you, driving you to further drink and deeper resentments. You cannot carry the burden of these sins, yet you try and keep on trying.

You interpret the loving acts of people around you as meddling and interference. You say your parents or your mate or others close to you are spying on you, are forcing you into a prison. You demand your freedom from them.

---

1. Proverbs 23:19-21, 29-34.

You are in a prison, beloved, but your loved ones have not placed you there. Not one of them has the power to do that. Not one of them is standing guard over you, not one is spying. You are a prisoner of Satan. He alone has the power to bring you such terrible enslavement, and he is watching every move you make.

You even resent inanimate objects. You fly into a rage if you so much as bump your head or stub your toe. You hurl the hammer against the wall if the nail doesn't go in just right. You honk your horn at the drivers ahead of you if they don't move fast enough to suit you. You curse and you rail and you rant. You pound the walls of the shower if the water runs cold. You kick the dog for no reason. You strike your children, you beat your mate. You shout, you scream. You argue without provocation. Always you do things for which you are sorry, but there is no way to express your sorrow . . . there is no way to expiate your guilt.

You develop unreasonable fears and things which you once faced with courage, you now hide from, terrorized that something is out there to get you. It's an awful feeling. There are no words to describe it.

You are overwhelmed with the sense of loss, and well you should be because the loss is very real. You are draining your purse and you regret it. You are losing the respect of your loved ones and you feel it. You demand they respect you, accept you as you are; but they cannot and deep in your heart you know that. Deep in your heart you don't blame them. You are losing your reputation and the burden of that is intolerable. You fear the loss of your job and for good reason: you are no longer a capable worker. You are not worthy of hire.

You have a growing sense of inadequacy. You feel debased and worthless. You experience the awful and very real feeling of failure. Everything you try to do turns sour.

And always there is that growing anxiety . . . that nameless dread with which you live and with which you cannot cope. You can't place your finger on that anxious feeling, you can't quite identify it, but it is there—growing, consuming. It is very real.

You are afraid for there is no security. Everything hangs in the balance. Your position is precarious. There is no one you can trust, no one who can secure your position. There is nothing to cling to anymore.

Where is that security you once felt? The confidence you once knew? Feelings of deep-seated inferiority overwhelm you. They gnaw away at every last shred of your sanity. Where will you turn?

I am aware of all these feelings. I am your God. I created you in My image and you were never meant to live like this. Do you think for one moment I don't understand what you're going through? The following words from the Bible describe the place you have reached in the depths of your misery:

" . . . my body is sick, my health is broken beneath my sins. They are like a flood, higher than my head; they are a burden too heavy to bear. My wounds are festering and full of pus. Because of my sins I am bent and racked with pain. My days are filled with anguish. My loins burn with inflammation and my whole body is diseased. I am exhausted and crushed; I groan in despair.

"Lord, you know how I long for my health once more. You hear my every sigh. My heart beats wildly, my strength fails, and I am going blind. My loved ones and friends stay away, fearing my disease. Even my own family stands at a distance.

"Meanwhile my enemies are trying to kill me. They plot my ruin and spend all their waking hours planning treachery.

"But I am deaf to all their threats; I am silent before them as a man who cannot speak. I have nothing to say, for I am waiting for you, O Lord my God. Come and protect me. Put an end to their arrogance, these who gloat when I am cast down!"[1]

---

1. Psalm 38. (TLB)

That enemy which is described is Satan, beloved. You cannot rid yourself of his influence by your own power. You have tried, have you not? Do you think for one moment I don't know that too? I am aware. Read again from My Word:

" . . . the trouble is not there [with the law of God] but with *me* because I am sold into slavery with Sin as my owner.

"I don't understand myself at all, for I really want to do what is right, but I can't. I do what I don't want to—what I hate. I know perfectly well that what I am doing is wrong, and my bad conscience proves that I agree with these laws I am breaking; but I can't help myself, because I'm no longer doing it. It is sin inside me that is stronger than I am that makes me do these evil things.

"I know I am rotten through and through so far as my old sinful nature is concerned. No matter which way I turn I can't make myself do right. I want to but I can't. When I want to do good, I don't; and when I try not to do wrong, I do it anyway. Now if I am doing what I don't want to, it is plain where the trouble is: sin . . . has me in its evil grasp."[1]

You see, I *do* understand. I *do* know. I *am* aware how you feel. And I want you to know I grieve for you, and if I were to express that grief in words, you couldn't comprehend them. But let Me assure you it is very great.

---

1. Romans 7:14-20. (TLB)

And let Me assure you I love you. Let Me assure you I have the answer for every problem you face! In Me you can regain your confidence. In Me you can find the security you have lost. I will carry each burden of resentment. I will cast away all your fears. I will remove all your anxiety, I will replace your hatred with love. I will create within you a new heart and a new spirit. I will set you free from the chains which bind you. I will take away your compulsion. I will give you peace. And I will do these things because "I am come that you might have life and have it more abundantly."[1]

I will satisfy that deep desire in your heart. I will quench your thirst for another drink because, you see, the true reason for your thirst is that your " . . . soul thirsteth for God."[2]

And will you ever thirst for alcohol again? No, for " . . . whosoever drinketh of the water that I shall give him shall never thirst . . . "[3]

Read on. Your salvation is near at hand. Your deliverance draweth nigh.

---

1. John 10:10.
2. Psalm 42:2.
3. John 4:14.

CHAPTER VII

Look At My Plan For Deliverance

Let Me tell you why you need a Savior.

I created man and woman perfect, whole and entire, wanting nothing. I created the earth over which I gave man dominion. To that first man, Adam, I gave a most precious gift: freedom. Adam had the freedom to accept or to reject My words to him, freedom to obey or disobey them, freedom to make himself happy or miserable.

As sons and daughters of Adam, you have that same freedom. Such a priceless gift is of extreme importance to you because there is a path that leads to destruction—that of Satan's. I did not create that path. It exists because of Satan and he is the ruler of darkness.

I wanted Adam to know joy in following Me. I wanted him to know life. I wanted him to dwell in the garden, rich with a supply of everything he would ever need.

He chose instead to listen to the tempter, and thus by "his offence, judgment came upon all men to condemnation."[1]

"But," some say, "that isn't fair. Why should we suffer because of what Adam did?"

You suffer because you, like Adam, have a choice and you have chosen wrongly. There isn't a day that goes by in which you don't have the choice either to follow Me or to follow Satan. I will not violate that freedom.

I forewarned Adam. I told him if he chose to follow evil he would die, yet he chose evil anyway. He chose to believe the voice of the tempter who said, "God doesn't mean that. Surely you won't die."

I have told you the same things. If you choose to sin, if you choose to worship Satan over Me— which is what you do when you follow him—you will die! You are well aware there are many people who choose to believe that God doesn't mean what He says in regard to that particular subject. "Surely we can do anything we please so long as we enjoy it," they say. "A loving God would never punish anyone. We all get enough hell on earth."

That's the voice of your tempter. Satan is real. Sin is real. Death is real, and you can't deny the existence of any one of these three.

All the ugliness, the violence, the tragedy and shame of everything you see in the world and in

---

1. Romans 5:18.

your life is the result of sin. Don't take it lightly.
Don't camouflage it by calling it simply human
weakness or mistaken judgment. Man chooses to
practice sin, and Satan seeks to delude man
about the consequences. You see, you can't
blame Satan for causing you to choose sin initial-
ly. He steps in once you yourself have made the
choice. And you can't blame your Creator either.
"Let no man say when he is tempted, I am
tempted of God; for God cannot be tempted with
evil, neither tempteth He any man. But every
man is tempted when he is DRAWN AWAY OF
HIS OWN LUST, and enticed. Then when lust
hath conceived, it bringeth forth sin; and sin,
when it is finished, bringeth forth death."[1]

I seek to reveal your sin to you and to save you
from it. And I have provided you with a Savior
because I love you as I love every man, woman
and child in *all* my creation. I want them *all* to
dwell with Me in everlasting peace and happiness.

Just exactly what is sin? It is lawlessness . . .
that is, it is the transgression of My law. I have
set the boundaries between good and evil; and
when you transgress those boundaries, you sin
against Me.

Sin is iniquity. That is, it is a deviation from
right action, whether or not a specific act is re-

---

1. James 1:13-15.

corded as forbidden. I have placed that knowledge within you and you know when you deviate from that which is good and moral and right. Iniquities are wrongs which spring from your own corrupt nature.

Sin is missing the mark, or falling short of the goal I have set for you; and that goal is to live as Christ has taught you.

Also, sin is trespassing into My divine authority and you have no right to do that. You place yourself above Me by rejecting My commandments to you and by following your ways instead of Mine. No man is above Me. No man is equal to Me. I have not set up arbitrary rules and regulations to take the joy out of your life but to give your life added joy. I have revealed these rules to you because I know what harm befalls you when you break them. It's that simple. I have explained these pitfalls to you because I love you, not because I delight in seeing you stumble and fall. I want to *keep* you from falling. I warn you just as loving parents warn their children of the things which will hurt and harm them.

Satan himself was at one time My angel. He thought he would be equal with Me, that he would rule over My creation. I cast him from heaven along with those angels who chose to follow him, and that's why he works his evil among those I love on earth. He hates Me and all My creation; but he will be free, just as you are free, until the day of judgment. Then he will be cast into the bottomless pit along with his followers. His desires are evil and until that final day, he will do everything in his power to get you to follow him. Those of you who choose to do so will follow him to eternal destruction, for My new heaven and new earth must be free of all those who work their abominations against Me.

That day is a long time coming you may say. My time is not your time and My ways are not your ways. Who are you to question them? I am not willing that any should perish. Perhaps I delay that day so that you alone will be set free. You cannot know the mind of God.

Choose not to follow Satan. You see, you are not wrestling against flesh and blood. If you were, you could overpower that evil one and destroy him. But you are wrestling " . . . against principalities, against powers, against the rulers of the darkness of this world, against spiritual wickedness in high places."[1]

Is it any wonder you're in the throes of such anguish? You're not playing with matches, beloved. You're wrestling against the most mighty, the most powerful, the most brilliant and sinister force of evil in the entire Universe! Satan. And he has a network of skilled assistants involved in such vast, intricate and ingenious machinations

1. Ephesians 6:12.

for evil as would make your most powerful crime syndicates look inept. What's more, you're a marked man or woman so far as he and his "mobsmen" are concerned and don't for one minute think otherwise.

You need a Savior to rescue you from those clutches. That's the reason I sent Jesus into the world. Only through His blood can you be set free from Satan and the power he has over you.

I sent Him into the world because I love you, and as your God, I am the source of love.

I want you to be restored so that there isn't a spot or a blemish or a stain on you. I want to clear your soul of all guilt so that you can be with Me in paradise. You can't begin to imagine what a wonderful place that will be because there will be no evil there whatsoever.

Christ came into the world that He might die. "He was manifested to take away your sins." [1] "Christ came into the world to give His life a ransom for many." [2]

"For God so loved the world He gave His only begotten Son, that whosoever believeth in Him should not perish but have everlasting life." [3]

There is no way for you to obtain salvation except through Jesus who said, "I am the way, the

---

1. I John 3:5.
2. Matthew 20:28.
3. John 3:16.

truth and the life. No man cometh unto the Father but by Me." [1]

You see, Jesus went every step of the way for you. He was God and became man for you. He lived among men to teach you about Me. He was tempted of Satan just as you are tempted, yet He did not sin. He suffered in your stead, He died in your stead. He descended into hell in your stead. And He rose into heaven that you might experience resurrection through Him. He sits at My right hand and He prays that you will seek the salvation He bought for you. He holds it out as a gift to you. He wants you to accept it.

You can't buy your salvation through good works. You can't suffer, die, descend into Hell and be raised again for your sins. . . . Christ had to do that for you and in so doing, He conquered death. He gave you victory over the grave. He gave you the assurance of everlasting life!

You have a debt you can't pay. That's why Christ paid it for you.

With His blood, He has redeemed those who come to Me through Him. " . . ye were not redeemed with corruptible things, as silver and gold, but with the precious blood of Christ, as of a lamb without blemish and spot." [2]

You see, there was nothing on earth which

---

1. John 14:6.
2. I Peter 1:19.

could have redeemed you. There was no man or woman righteous enough. There was nothing on earth that was eternal, perfect, whole, without blemish or stain.

You needed to be redeemed by Perfection unto perfection. You needed to be reedemed by Glory unto glory. You needed to be redeemed by your Creator because no other power could purchase salvation for you.

When you chose drinking to excess as your way of life, you chose Satan as your God, and he is destroying your body, soul and spirit. He will keep at you until the destruction is total, complete and eternal.

Does Satan give you joy? Does he offer you security? Does he offer you peace in your mind and peace in your household? Does he offer you health? Wisdom? Protection? Happiness? Does he offer you deliverance? Salvation? Eternal life?

Do you *want* deliverance? Then "Come unto Me, all ye that weary and are heavy laden and I will give you rest."[1]

How do you come unto Me? My way is so simple wise men can't understand it. You simply repent of your sins, turn from them, ask for forgiveness through the blood of Jesus, and you will be cleansed from all unrighteousness.

That simple you ask? How can that be? Should I have had a more complex plan? One

---

1. Matthew 11:28.

you couldn't understand? One you had to work at for many years? Should I have required perfection of you? Should I have asked you to enlist an army of the world's mightiest men for the purpose of annihilating Satan and his kingdom? Should I have asked for your silver and gold? Could you amass a fortune to pay for paradise? To pay for the suffering and death of My Son?

No. Salvation must be free. You are saved by My grace "through faith and that not of yourselves, it is a gift of God, not of works, lest any man should boast." [1]

Simply do your part and I will do Mine.

"If you confess your sins, I am faithful and just to forgive you your sins and to cleanse you from all unrighteousness." [2]

I will declare you NOT GUILTY. Do you know what that means? It means you will be just as though you had never sinned. Think of it!

No matter how low you have sunk, no matter how hopeless your condition has become, no matter how many people you have hurt, no matter what sins you have committed, you will be declared NOT GUILTY by reason of the cross on which Jesus died!

"And since by His blood I did all this for you as sinners, how much more will I do for you now that I have declared you not guilty? Now I will

---

1. Ephesians 2:8-9.
2. I John 1:9.

save you from all My wrath to come." [1]

When will you be delivered?

Upon your confession of sin and faith in Jesus Christ and not one second later. Right now, as a matter of truth, for many who have read these words and have made their confession just moments ago.

There is rejoicing in Heaven right now! The angels are singing their praises because one man, having been a drunkard for over thirty years, just made the decision to let Christ be the Lord of his life. They're singing because yet another made that decision, and another. They're singing this moment because a young mother just called out for her deliverance. When these people stand before Me on the day of judgment, I will bid them enter My heavenly kingdom because on that day, I will open the Lamb's Book of Life and find their names written there.

Others will read these words, yet they will not come; and on that day I will grieve when I tell them, "Depart from Me, ye cursed, into everlasting fire prepared for the devil and his angels." [2]

Let Me quote from Jesus' words. Read and claim your promise.

"Truly, truly, I say to you, he who believes has eternal life." [3]

---

1. Romans 5:8-9. (TLB)
2. Matthew 25:41.
3. John 6:47.

"I say emphatically that anyone who listens to My message and believes in God who sent Me has eternal life, and will never be damned for his sins, but HAS ALREADY PASSED OUT OF DEATH INTO LIFE." [1]

And no one can take you out of My kingdom from the moment you accept Me on. Not any man or woman. Not Satan. Not any or all of his angels. "My sheep hear My voice, and I know them, and they follow Me: and I give unto them eternal life: and they shall never perish, NEITHER SHALL ANY MAN PLUCK THEM OUT OF MY HAND." [2]

"These things have I written unto you who believe in the name of the Son of God, IN ORDER THAT YOU MAY KNOW THAT YOU HAVE ETERNAL LIFE." [3]

There are many wonders in store for those who accept Me. "Christ came with this new agreement so that all who are invited may come AND HAVE FOREVER ALL THE WONDERS GOD HAS PROMISED THEM!" [4]

You're invited. Will you come?

One of the wonders in store for you is that I WILL REBUILD THE TEMPLE! Can you believe that? Test Me. Try Me. Prove Me and see if

1. John 5:24. (TLB)
2. John 10:27-28.
3. I John 5:13.
4. Hebrews 9:15. (TLB)

I won't pour out unmeasured blessings on you here and now! I long to give you every good thing, and I will restore you in body, soul and spirit.

CHAPTER VIII

I Will Rebuild the Temple

"From today . . . and from this day onward, I will bless you. Notice, I am giving you this promise now before you have even begun to rebuild the temple . . . From *this* day I will bless you."[1]

The principle upon which I would work in you, My temple, can be found in those verses from My Word as they appear in Haggai. The reference is made to Zerubbabel, once governor of Judah, to whom I gave a message through My prophet Haggai. The people of that land dwelt in luxurious homes and had every blessing, but they let My temple lie in ruins. I held back the rains, their crops withered, yet they refused to worship Me. They ignored My temple.

But Zerubbabel was faithful as was Joshua, the High Priest, and a few of the people remaining in that land. They obeyed My message from Haggai and began to worship Me in earnest.

It was then I sent them word, "I am with you;

---

1. Haggai 2:18, 19. (TLB)

97

I will bless you . . . and I gave them a desire to rebuild My temple . . . " [1]

And when they began the actual work of rebuilding, I sent another message to Zerubbabel through My prophet:

"Who among you can remember the temple as it was before? How glorious it was! In comparison, it is nothing now, is it? But take courage . . . take courage and work, for I am with you . . . so don't be afraid . . . In just a little while . . . I will fill this place with My glory . . . THE FUTURE SPLENDOR OF THIS TEMPLE WILL BE GREATER THAN THE SPLENDOR OF THE FIRST ONE! For I have plenty of silver and gold to do it! And here I will give peace." [2]

You can apply that message to your life right now and I will bless *you*. If you have come to Me through Jesus Christ, and if you begin now to worship Me in earnest, I will even give you the *desire* to rebuild the temple which is your body, soul and spirit! And I will bless your efforts for I can supply all you need to do it!

Remember how it was before you began drinking? Do you recall how great that body felt? Think about that for a moment and then consider this: if you take courage and work, I will fill your temple with glory so that your future will be

1. Haggai 1:13-15. (TLB)
2. Haggai 2:3-9. (TLB)

far greater than the very best of the past you remember!

This is My promise to you and I guarantee I will fulfill it so long as you do your part.

You see, you don't even have to have the desire on your own. Worship Me in earnest and I'll even give *that* to you.

Now you feel that your life lies in ruins—and indeed it does—but take heart, for the excitement is about to begin! My glory is about to be revealed in you!

You see, " . . . you *are* My workmanship,"[1] which means I'm not finished with you yet. I am still in the business of creating just as I was when I first fashioned you. "It was I who covered you in your mother's womb. Abide in Me and you will praise Me, for you are fearfully and wonderfully made! Marvellous are My works . . . your substance was not hid from Me when you were made in secret and curiously wrought in the lowest parts of the earth. My eyes did see your substance, yet being unperfect; and in My book all your members were written, which in continuance were fashioned, when as yet there were none of them."[2]

Don't be despondent for the way you are at this moment in time. "Shall the thing formed say to him that formed it, 'Why hast thou made me

---

1. Ephesians 2:10.
2. Psalm 139:13-16.

thus?' "[1]

"Woe unto him that striveth with his Maker!
. . . Shall the clay say to him that fashioneth it,
'What makest thou?' or thy work, 'He hath no
hands?' "[2]

You see, I'm the designer and I will make you
as a perfect jewel in My sight, so be patient.
Trust Me. Serve Me. I know what's best for you.

"And you shall be Mine . . . in that day when
I make up My jewels; and I will spare you as a
man spareth his own son that serveth him."[3]

Let Me tell you those things which I will do
for you as we work together in the task of restoring the ruins and rebuilding that temple which is
your body, your spirit and your soul—the latter
comprising your mind, will and emotions.

I WILL TAKE AWAY YOUR GUILT AND
YOUR GUILT FEELINGS! "There is therefore
now no condemnation for those who are in Christ
Jesus."[4]

"Everyone who trusts in Me is freed from all
guilt and declared righteous—something the
Jewish law could never do."[5]

"Who dares accuse you whom I have chosen
for My own? Will I? No! I am the one who has

1. Romans 9:20.
2. Isaiah 45:9.
3. Malachi 3:17.
4. Romans 8:1.
5. Acts 13:39. (TLB)

forgiven you and given you right standing with Myself.[1]

"Who then will condemn you? Will Christ? No! For He is the one who died for you and came back to life again for you and is sitting at the place of highest honor next to Me, pleading for you here in heaven."[2]

You see, when I blotted out your sins, I cast them from My memory. I don't remember them anymore. "I, even I, am the one who wipes out your transgressions for My own sake; and I WILL NOT REMEMBER YOUR SINS."[3]

"As far as the east is from the west, so far have I removed your transgressions from you."[4]

"I've blotted out your sins; they are gone like morning mist at noon."[5]

"No matter how deep the stain of your sins, I can take it out and make you as clean as freshly fallen snow. Even if you are stained as red as crimson, I can make you white as wool."[6]

So now that you've come to Me, there is no reason for you to hang guilt trips on yourself for past actions. If I have so forgiven you, you have the right and the responsibility to forgive yourself. You've got to let the guilt feelings go. Satan

---

1. Romans 8:33. (TLB)
2. *Ibid.*, 34.
3. Isaiah 43:25.
4. Psalm 103:12.
5. Isaiah 44:22. (TLB)
6. Isaiah 1:18. (TLB)

would like it if you hung on to them but you must not. When you let them go, "What happiness for those whose guilt has been forgiven! What joys when sins are covered over! What relief for those who have confessed their sins and I have cleared their record." [1]

I WILL GIVE YOU A CLEAR CONSCIENCE! Ask forgiveness of those you have wronged. You know who they are. Be truly sorry for those things which you have done against others; and if it is possible, go to each person and ask forgiveness for those things. "He that covereth his sins shall not prosper, but whoso confesseth and forsaketh them shall have mercy." [2]

"If thou bring thy gift to the altar and there rememberest that thy brother hath ought against thee, leave there thy gift by the altar and go thy way. First be reconciled to thy brother, then come again and offer thy gift." [3]

It's very important to ask those you've offended the most for their forgiveness first. If you don't, you'll find it difficult to have a clear conscience and to feel the freedom from guilt which I've given you. Perhaps you need to ask your wife to forgive you, your husband, your children, your parents, your brothers and sisters. These are the people closest to you. Tell them you're sorry for

1. Psalm 32:1, 2. (TLB)
2. Proverbs 28:13.
3. Matthew 5:23-24.

the way you treated them, identify the wrongs, and tell them that with My help you don't intend to treat them like that anymore. Ask them to forgive you. Perhaps you'll be broken hearted when you remember the harm and hurt and disappointment your offenses have brought these loved ones; but if you confess those things, I will heal your broken heart.

You need not review the ugly details of your sins. In fact, it's better that you do not. "It is a shame even to speak of those things which are done of them in secret."[1] The important thing is that you let your loved one know you're aware of the offense, that you're aware you were wrong, and that you want forgiveness and the chance to make what restitution you can. You must then trust My spirit to take care of the rest.

When you've done that—and it won't be as difficult as you imagine—you will know what peace there is in having your conscience cleared.

I would then ask that you forgive all those who have wronged *you*. When you're resentful, when you're bitter, you want revenge toward the person who has offended you. You want to punish that person. But you must remember that " . . . vengeance is Mine,"[2] it is never yours. "I will repay,"[3] and that will take care of it. Even if

---

1. Ephesians 5:12.
2. Romans 12:19.
3. *Ibid.*

someone has wronged you time and time again I ask you to forgive. Read the account of the servant in Matthew 18:21-35, and you will understand why forgiveness is so important. The servant asked Jesus how many times he should forgive someone who wronged him. "Would seven times be enough?"

"No," replied Jesus, "not seven times, but seventy times seven!" In other words, you always forgive. The story is told in that scripture of the King who cancelled the debt of a servant who asked for leniency. And then, when that same servant found one of his friends who owed him a few shillings, he seized that person and cried, "Pay up what you owe me."

The fellow-servant then implored him (as he earlier had implored the King), "Be patient with me and I will pay you back."

But the servant refused and had him thrown in prison. Then the King said to him, "You wicked servant. Didn't I cancel all that debt when you begged me to do so? Oughtn't you to have taken pity on your fellow-servant as I, your master, took pity on you?" And his master in anger handed him over to the jailers until he should repay the whole debt. This is how your Heavenly Father will treat you unless you forgive your brothers from your heart.

You see, when you harbor bitterness toward another, you're measuring yourself by that person's actions, thus assuming your superiority to him. I've warned you against this sort of thing in My Word. " . . . but they measuring themselves by themselves, and comparing themselves among themselves are not wise." [1]

By asking forgiveness of those you have wronged and by forgiving those who have wronged you, you will have a clear conscience, and that is a necessary ingredient for the restoration of your temple.

What else will I do for you? I WILL MAKE YOUR ENEMIES TO BE AT PEACE WITH YOU. "When your ways please the Lord, I make even those who are against you to be at peace with you." [2]

I WILL HEAL YOUR BROKEN HEART. "I will heal the broken in heart and bind up their wounds." [3]

"I will comfort your hearts with all comfort, and help you in every good thing you say and do." [4]

"The Lord has comforted His people, and will have compassion upon them in their sorrow." [5]

"I, even I, am He who comforts you." [6]

---

1. II Corinthians 10:12.
2. Proverbs 16:7.
3. Psalm 147:3.
4. II Thessalonians 2:16, 17. (TLB)
5. Isaiah 49:13. (TLB)
6. Isaiah 51:12. (TLB)

"Blessed are they that mourn: for they shall be comforted." [1]

"I know the number of hairs on your head! Never fear, you are far more valuable to Me than a whole flock of sparrows." [2]

"The Lord is near to the broken hearted, and saves those who are crushed in spirit." [3]

I WILL GIVE YOU HAPPINESS! "Happy is he whose transgression is forgiven, whose sin is covered . . ." [4]

"The righteous shall be glad in the Lord, and shall trust in Him; and all the upright in heart shall glory." [5]

"You will go out with joy, and be led forth with peace.[6]

"Happy is the man who puts his trust in the Lord." [7]

"You shall rejoice all the day, and by My righteousness you are exalted." [8]

"You shall rejoice in all the good which the Lord your God has given you and your household." [9]

---

1. Matthew 5:4.
2. Luke 12:7.
3. Psalm 34:18.
4. Psalm 32:1.
5. Psalm 64:10.
6. Isaiah 55:12.
7. Proverbs 16:20. (TLB)
8. Psalm 89:16.
9. Deuteronomy 26:11.

"Therefore you will joyously draw water from the springs of salvation." [1]

I WILL GIVE YOU STRENGTH! "I will seek that which was lost, and bring again that which was driven away, and will bind up that which was broken, and will strengthen that which was sick." [2]

"They that wait upon the Lord shall renew their strength; they shall mount up with wings as eagles. They shall run and not be weary, they shall walk and not faint." [3]

I WILL TAKE AWAY YOUR FEARS! "For I have not given you the spirit of fear; but of power, and of love and of a sound mind." [4]

"There is no fear in love; but perfect love casteth out fear because fear hath torment. He that feareth is not made perfect in love." [5]

"Fear not, for I am with you. Do not be dismayed. I am your God. I will strengthen you; I will help you; I will uphold you with My victorious right hand." [6]

"You shall not be afraid of evil tidings: your heart is fixed, trusting in the Lord." [7]

---

1. Isaiah 12:3.
2. Ezekiel 34:16.
3. Isaiah 40:31.
4. II Timothy 1:7.
5. I John 4:18.
6. Isaiah 41:10. (TLB)
7. Psalm 112:7.

I WILL GIVE YOU PEACE! "Peace I leave with you, My peace I give unto you . . . not as the world giveth, give I unto you. Let not your heart be troubled, neither let it be afraid."[1]

"When your anxious thoughts multiply within you, My consolations will delight your soul."[2]

"You will experience My peace, which is far more wonderful than the human mind can understand. My peace will keep your thoughts and your hearts quiet and at rest as you trust in Christ Jesus."[3]

"I will keep in perfect peace all those who trust in Me whose thoughts turn often to the Lord."[4]

I WILL GIVE YOU FREEDOM! "It is to freedom that you have been called . . . only be careful that freedom does not become mere opportunity for your lower nature. You should be free to serve each other in love."[5]

"You shall know the truth and the truth will set you free!"[6]

"For the power of the life-giving Spirit—and this power is yours through Jesus—has freed you from the vicious circle of sin and death."[7]

---

1. John 14:27.
2. Psalm 94:19.
3. Philippians 4:7. (TLB)
4. Isaiah 26:3. (TLB)
5. Galatians 5:13.
6. John 8:32.
7. Romans 8:2. (TLB)

"I WILL GIVE YOU SAFETY AND SUC-CESS IN ALL YOU DO! "I have made an ever-lasting covenant with you; My agreement is eter-nal, final, sealed. I will constantly look after your safety and success!" [1]

"Then you shall prosper, if you are careful to observe the statutes and the ordinances which the Lord commanded Moses concerning Israel. Be strong and courageous, do not fear nor be dis-mayed." [2]

"In everything you do, put Me first and I will direct you and crown your efforts with success." [3]

"As long as you seek the Lord, I make you to prosper." [4]

"No evil will befall you, nor will any plague come near your tent." [5]

I WILL GIVE YOU WISDOM! "If any of you lacks wisdom, let him ask of Me who gives to all men generously and without reproach, and it will be given to him." [6]

"For I give those who please Me wisdom, knowledge and joy."[7]

"The fear of the Lord is the beginning of wis-

---

1. II Samuel 23:5. (TLB)
2. I Chronicles 22:13.
3. Proverbs 3:6. (TLB)
4. II Chronicles 26:5.
5. Psalm 91:10.
6. James 1:5.
7. Ecclesiastes 2:26. (TLB)

dom: and the knowledge of the holy is understanding." [1]

"I WILL GIVE YOU PATIENCE! "Rest in the Lord; wait patiently for Him to act. Don't be envious of evil men who prosper. For the wicked shall be destroyed, but those who trust in the Lord shall be given every blessing." [2]

"Better is the end of a thing than the beginning thereof; and the patient in spirit is better than the proud in spirit." [3]

"Do not throw away your confidence, which has a great reward. For yet a very little while, he who is coming will come, and will not delay." [4]

"And let us not get tired of doing what is right, for after a while you will reap a harvest of blessing if you don't get discouraged and give up." [5]

I WILL RESTORE YOUR MIND! I will give you the mind which was in Christ Jesus. " . . . and be renewed in the spirit of your mind; and that ye put on the new man, which after Me is created in righteousness and true holiness." [6]

I WILL RESTORE YOUR BODY! "I will give you back your health again and heal your

---

1. Proverbs 9:10.
2. Psalm 37:7-9. (TLB)
3. Ecclesiastes 7:8.
4. Hebrews 10:35, 37.
5. Galatians 6:9. (TLB)
6. Ephesians 4:23, 24.

wounds." [1]

"The Lord will sustain you upon your sickbed; in your illness, I do restore you to health." [2]

"These troubles and sufferings of yours are, after all, quite small and won't last very long. Yet this short time of distress will result in My richest blessing upon you forever and ever." [3]

" . . . your recovery will speedily spring forth . . . " [4]

"I will bring you health and cure . . . " [5]

"He personally carried the load of your sins in His own body when He died on the cross, so that you can be finished with sin and live a good life from now on. For His wounds have healed yours!" [6]

"I, the Lord, am your healer." [7]

I WILL CARE FOR YOUR LOVED ONES! "I will give them one heart, and one way, that they may fear Me forever, for the good of them, and of their children after them." [8]

"The Lord shall increase you more and more, you *and* your children." [9]

---

1. Jeremiah 30:17. (TLB)
2. Psalm 41:3.
3. II Corinthians 4:17. (TLB)
4. Isaiah 58:8.
5. Jeremiah 33:6.
6. I Peter 2:24. (TLB)
7. Exodus 15:26.
8. Jeremiah 32:39.
9. Psalm 115:14.

"You shall rejoice in all the good which I have given you *and* your household."[1]

You see, there isn't one good thing which I will withhold from those who love Me and serve Me. I will rebuild the temple of your body, soul and spirit so that it is entirely new and men shall see My glory in you, and shall marvel at My works. "If any man be in Christ he *is* a new creature. Old things *are* passed away. Behold, *all* things *are* become new!"[2]

There are many people who have an awfully warped view of what this business of being a Christian is all about. Don't listen to them. Trust *Me*. You're about to enter into the most exciting adventure, the most exhilarating experience of your life!

Review those things which I just promised you. All this I'll give you and heaven too! What more could you ask? (If you should think of anything, just let Me know and I'll supply that too . . . provided it's good for you, of course.)

Are you still an alcoholic? NO! You are a sinner saved by grace and all old things are now passed away.

Will your compulsion for alcohol disappear? YES! If you abide in Me.

Can Satan bring you back into his clutches? NO! You are Mine from this day forward. And

---

1. Deuteronomy 26:11.

2. II Corinthians 5:17.

". . . no mere man has ever seen, heard or even imagined what wonderful things I have ready for those who love the Lord." [1]

Can you still be tempted to drink? Yes, but if you abide in Me, I will give you the power to resist the temptation!

---

1. I Corinthians 2:9. (TLB)

CHAPTER IX

What To Do When You're Tempted

You will be strengthened if you seek the fellowship of people who understand the particular kind of stress you face should the desire for a drink arise. Regular association with them will be invaluable to you if they're the kind of people who focus on victory instead of defeat. These should be people who are free from condemnation and live as though they were . . . people who aren't self-righteous but who refrain at all times from judging others for anything whatsoever . . . people who accept My Word for what it means and who live as though every promise in it is absolutely and eternally true for indeed My Word is truth. In other words, I would have you associate with people who know what it means to live in Christ, to have their being in Christ and who live with the joy that kind of life gives them.

It won't help you to associate with people who believe you must abstain from drinking using your own power alone, or people who believe you'll have to fight this problem the rest of your life. It won't help if they continually focus on the past and past problems with alcohol . . . if they relate experiences ad infinitum of drunken behavior and its consequences. These things belabor the evil of what was once a part of your life and draws it all back into your consciousness.

When I ask you to abstain from all appearance of evil, I certainly do include this sort of thing. When you focus on past behavior, you remind yourself to be tempted and most likely you'll find such temptation too difficult to overcome.

Forget the past! Would you spend your life groveling in refuse heaps? When you throw out your garbage and the collector hauls it away, do you follow the truck to the dump so that you can go through it all again? Do you make a daily pilgrimage there to look at it? Of course not. Do you haul it back into your home so that it can rot and decay and defile your dwelling? Of course not. How much more important not to do such a thing with your mind!

Remember, you're free. You're delivered. I have removed the transgressions of your past behavior as far as the east is from the west. I've forgotten those things. Ask Me to call them to mind and I won't be able to. I don't gather groups of saints together in heaven so that we can discuss all the folly of their past transgressions. We don't sit around and go over the details of what so and so is doing wrong. What a waste of time! What foolish activity!

You now have your being in eternity, remember that. You always have had; and since you've accepted your deliverance, live as though you're delivered *now* for indeed you are!

Stop reviewing your past. Stop tempting yourself. Words are powerful things. "Either you will be justified by them or you will be condemned."[1] Your words, then, can and do reflect your fate.

Remember, you make use of words not only when you express something in the presence of others, but also when you let your mind dwell on certain thoughts. You "think" with words, do you not?

Remember these truths from My Word, commit them to memory and express them aloud when you're tempted to discuss your past behavior with others, or to reflect upon your present inclinations to slip back into old behavior patterns:

"Pleasant words are as an honeycomb, sweet to the soul, and health to the bones!"[2]

"He who guards his mouth and his tongue guards his soul from troubles."[3]

"He that will love life, and see good days, let

---

1. Matthew 12:37. (TLB)
2. Proverbs 16:24.
3. Proverbs 21:23.

him refrain his tongue from evil, and his lips that they speak no guile." [1]

Keep affirming these truths until they become ingrained in your mind . . . until they become such a part of you they'll spring forth automatically when you have need of them.

Just as you before practiced your destructive habit, so now I would have you practice the art of living in Me. Just as before your practice led you into bondage, your new practices will lead you into freedom.

And in time you'll see you're making progress. There'll come a day you'll realize you no longer have any desire to drink. There'll come a day you'll have health throughout your body, and your mind and soul will no longer be bowed down by troubles.

As you practice, discipline yourself to set aside a quiet time to be alone with Me each day. During this period, read further into My Word, meditate on it; then be still and know that I am God. Quiet yourself before Me every time you feel you're being drawn away. Call to Me in prayer. Believe that I will hear you for I do. Believe that I will give you victory because I will. Believe that I am near for indeed My Spirit dwells within you.

---

1. I Peter 3:10.

Consider thoughts of temptation as your adversaries and ponder this truth: "For I will give you the right words and such logic and none of your opponents [adversaries] will be able to reply!"[1]

When you're tempted, talk to Me! Tell Me everything. Remember, I'm your best friend. I'm your divine physician, your divine psychiatrist, your divine counselor. I have the answers to *all* your questions and the solutions for *all* your problems. When you call to Me in prayer, realize you are consciously focusing My healing power along specific constructive lines! This power heals disease, solves problems, renews your physical being and charges you with an energy and strength far above and beyond your ordinary capacity to do these things for yourself. PRAYER IS POWER!

Realize that while you're unique as an individual, your temptations and problems aren't unique. Nothing can come your way that I haven't handled or that I can't handle. I'll help you to overcome all things if you trust Me.

"There hath no temptation taken you but such as is common to man. But God is able and will not suffer you to be tempted above that which you are able but will, with the temptation,

1. Luke 21:15. (TLB)

also provide a way of escape that you may be able to bear it."[1]

Commit that verse to memory. It has a promise you should claim every time you feel yourself slipping. You see, you don't have to be drawn away by temptations because I've promised you a way of escape every time one comes your way. Not just once, not just now and then, but EVERY SINGLE TIME! Believe that, test it and you'll get downright excited when you see the miraculous ways I'll provide your escape routes!

A lot of people interpret that scripture to mean that because I've provided escapes, I've also provided temptations. That's ridiculous. I've told you I cannot be tempted and that I don't tempt any man. If you have a picture in your mind that I'm the kind of God who sits in heaven and throws temptations in front of man and then becomes outraged because man succumbs to them, dismiss it right now! I know all things. Surely you must realize I know what you're going to do in each situation. Why would I hurl stones in your path to see if you might surprise Me and stumble on one now and then? Come now, give Me credit for more sense than that!

Truly I get weary of such distorted views. I would ask those people who harbor them this

---

1. I Corinthians 10:13.

question: What parent in his right mind would deliberately set traps for his children, then hide in some obscure spot to watch as they stumble into them? And then take great delight in punishing those children for falling?

Parents do what they can to make the way clear for their children. They do everything in their power to assure their safety. Their desires are that those children possess and experience every good thing.

If you know how to give good things to your children, don't you think your Heavenly Father knows how also? I wish above *all* things that you will prosper and be in good health. I'm *able* to give you all good things and I've given you the key to secure them. I'm all powerful, all knowing and everywhere present. Surely you must realize I can give you the power to overcome the temptation to drink. " . . . greater is He who is in you than he who is in the world."[1] Remember that whenever you're drawn away of your own lust and desire a drink.

You see, the entire key to living victoriously as opposed to struggling with temptations and as opposed to merely existing, is to BE that which you are: A CHILD OF GOD! It's one thing to know it, quite another to BE it . . . but that's where the good part is . . . that's where the joy is!

---

1. I John 4:4.

Many Christians live defeated lives because they haven't caught on to this BE-ing business. That's the secret to overcoming temptation and to receiving all the good things which I have in store for you.

Notice the words in the following scripture, meditate on them, commit them to memory and claim the promise by affirming it for yourself every time temptation comes upon you: "If any man BE in Christ, he IS a new creature. OLD THINGS ARE PASSED AWAY, behold, ALL things ARE BECOME NEW!"[1]

Believe that, affirm that, and you won't have any trouble resisting temptation. You'll put the devil on the run. He's not all powerful, he's not all knowing, and he's not able to stay where I'm in charge, so realize the power that's on your side. "Resist the devil and he will flee from you."[2]

Resist by using My armor "whenever the enemy attacks, and when it is all over, you will still be standing up."[3]

If you're afraid you'll slip and fall and take counsel of those fears, then the thing which you greatly fear will come upon you. So fear not because I am with you. You don't have a single thing to worry about!

---

1. II Corinthians 5:17.
2. James 4:7. (TLB)
3. Ephesians 6:13.

Let's review those points I've stressed to give you victory over temptation:

1. Seek fellowship with victorious people.
2. Read My Word and meditate upon it.
3. Draw yourself away quietly and listen to the voice of My Spirit within you.
4. Pray in every situation and without ceasing.
5. Claim My promises to you by affirming them and acting upon them.
6. Avoid all words and thoughts which concentrate on your old ways.
7. Resist the enemy and he will flee from you.
8. Trust Me to provide avenues of escape for every temptation that arises.
9. Refuse to take counsel of your fears.
10. BE!

Remember, you want living water, not poison; and should you ever think of poisoning yourself again, reread this chapter. Or consider this affirmation by writer E. Holmes. It will remind you who you are:

> My body is a spiritual laboratory where all I think, say and do is transformed from [God's] substance of life into health, vitality and energy.
> . . . Wisely I understand that hate, anger, resentment and revenge are self-punishing, distilling poisons that corrode the system into disease and decay.
> . . . My body is no older than my thinking . . . My body is no cleaner than my think-

ing. Therefore, every day I put on a new body by correct thinking. My blood stream is pure and fresh as the thought stream is cleansed and refreshed.

Mentally, spiritually the fountain of life plays through every organ function and gland of my being. There is no retention of waste tissues, congested accumulations, no old, unhappy memories. The joints are easy and flexible. There are no deposits. There is no high or low pressure. There is just peace, harmony and freedom in every department of my being.

I breathe deeply; I think joyously . . . My body is the temple of the living God, the temple of living love and radiant life. [His] Spirit animates every organ, gland and function of it. Health, strength, and vitality glow through every particle of it. The entire manifestation of [God's] Spirit, both visible and invisible, is the body of God.

As that affirmation applies to the temple of your body, so shall it apply to your life!

BE!

CHAPTER X

Words of Advice to Your Loved Ones

If you've read the preceding chapters, you know your loved one isn't the victim of a disease. He's caught up in sin. Therefore, you must not treat him as though he were sick and feel sorry for him. You can't nurse him back to health and you shouldn't expect that you can. Of yourself, you are powerless in the matter because you can't deliver any man or woman from sin. Only I can do that.

Knowing that shouldn't give you cause to despair, but rather it should give you hope, for there is much you can do to help yourself, your loved one and your family to find the victory over this present turmoil.

Remember, too, that no matter how your loved one acts when he's drinking, no matter how aware you are that he's guilty of error, you must avoid all temptation to sit in judgment of him! Neither are you to assume that you're more righteous than he.

It's not up to you to "convict" him or her by pronouncing sentence upon him. You're not to attempt being that person's conscience by giving your interpretations of his wrongs no matter how bad they seem to you. He has a perfectly good conscience of his own in the first place; and in the second place, who are you to judge his actions? And who are you to mete out punishment as though you know what's best in the way of discipline? Remember, vengeance is mine. It's never yours. You're not to sit in judgment of the alcoholic or of anyone else. Neither are you to condemn any individual. Leave the convicting to Me; and as far as condemning is concerned, there won't be any need for condemnation if your loved one turns to Christ which is what your true goal for him should be.

That doesn't mean you must condone what the alcoholic is doing. Far from it. You must refuse to be a party to his sin no matter what it costs. And you must confront him or her with his wrong doing by stating the facts of it.

The reason for that must be clear to you. You see, your loved one has developed a keen defense system of denial and rationalization, and thus he's grossly self-deluded. He doesn't deal with himself realistically. That's why you can't communicate with him on a rational level, and most certainly not on an emotional level. He may have black-outs and thus not remember his behavior.

Alcohol has dulled his brain so that he can't remember specific details of his actions.

The only defense that seems plausible to him is to deny he did such and so or that he said such and so. Naturally you'll want to interpret such statements as outright lies, and they are, but your alcoholic doesn't perceive them as lies. If you accuse him of lying, then, you'll only make him more defensive.

You must simply state the truth of his actions in love. Facts, not opinions or accusations, are what will ultimately help you break through that barrier of denial he's erected.

"You shall know the truth and the truth shall set you free." [1]

You can be My channel in revealing truth to the alcoholic if you will present your statements simply and non-judgmentally. Your loved one, remember, will hear the facts even though you may think he's not listening, but he'll tune out anything else you may say.

If he stumbled into the table and broke a lamp, for example, present him with that fact and that fact alone. No matter how upset you are, no matter how prized your possession was, calmly tell him the next morning, or whenever he sobers up, "You stumbled into the table last night and broke the lamp."

1. John 8:32.

Then let the matter drop! Walk away if you have to, but don't permit him or her to drag you into argument about it or to hurl some accusation at you to take you off guard and put you into a position where you start defending yourself in some other matter. Alcoholics are past masters at that sort of thing.

Don't attack his character by calling him clumsy or stupid. His opinion of himself is low enough already. Don't nag. Don't weep. Don't rant or rave or scream. State the fact and let it go. He'll get the message.

If you jump in there ready to do battle, ready to make a scene, you'll say things you'll wish you hadn't said, make threats you won't be able to carry out and shut the door you've opened. My Spirit won't be heard above the din.

Whatever you do, don't cover up your loved one's actions by ignoring them or by making excuses for them. When you do these things you're standing in My way. You're hindering the work I would perform in that person.

Yet another hindrance to My working with your loved one is for you to take that person's responsibilities away from him. Remember, you must not be a party to his sin. If you're asked to call the employer to say your mate's ill and can't come to work—and the truth is that he's either hanging one on or sleeping one off—you are not to make the call. That's *his* responsibility.

If he asks you to buy him liquor, you are to refuse to do so. You must not be a party to his sin. If he asks you to serve him liquor, you are to refuse. If he asks you to accompany him to a function where he will be drinking, you are to refuse to go. You should refuse to engage in *any* activity which indulges him in his sin and accompanying distorted fantasies, and don't despair if you're reproved for your actions. You probably will be. You must remember that I am with you.

If you are abiding in Me, I will not permit your trial to be more than you can bear. I will give My " . . . angels charge of you, to guard you in all your ways. On their hands they will bear you up, lest you dash your foot against a stone." [1]

If you abide in Me, you can " . . . rejoice though now for a season if need be if you are in heaviness . . . that the trial of your faith be much more precious than of gold that perisheth. Though it be tried with fire, it will be found unto praise and honor and glory at the appearing of Jesus Christ." [2]

Remember too, you are not to permit yourself to be blamed for the drinking of another. You're not to be a scapegoat for anybody. It's natural for sinners to blame others for their actions. They don't like the weight of their burdens, and they

---

1. Psalm 91:11-12.
2. I Peter 1:6-7.

don't realize Christ is the only one who can carry those burdens. If you take on another person's guilt, you're being highly presumptuous so far as your God is concerned. You see, since you can't sin for another, there's no way you can pay the price of sin for another either.

Each man is responsible for his own actions and is accountable to Me for them. You stay out of it.

I would also have you study My Word. Meditate upon it day and night. It will be " . . . a lamp unto your feet and a light unto your path." [1]

I would have you pray without ceasing, remembering as you pray that " . . . the Lord hears the good man when he calls to him for help and saves him out of all his troubles." [2]

I would have you seek the fellowship of Christian friends. They will help you in time of need and give you comfort and encouragement along the way. But don't use those friends as a sounding board so that you can berate your loved one in front of them. Behold the Christ in your alcoholic at all times, and let those friends remind you to do so when you forget.

Whatever you do, don't withdraw from others. Don't try to handle your burdens alone. You need the companionship of My people, and

---

1. Psalm 119:105.
2. Psalm 34:17. (TLB)

it is no disgrace to seek it. Seek out those who understand and can offer you consul in the light of My Word. If there are friends who would confront your alcoholic with the truth in love, by all means encourage them to do so. It's the most kind, courageous and loving thing they could do for him and for you. Far too often friends elect to stay out of it and go their way hoping something good might happen. If they'd speak up, if they'd go to that suffering one—without fear of losing his friendship, without fear of what the sufferer might think or say or do—if they'd tell that person, "Look, your drinking is destroying your life and you need to seek help in the name of Christ," they would help My cause immensely and give you great encouragement besides.

I would advise them to go collectively, at least in two's, though there may come times when an individual can do much on his own.

This business of waiting patiently for the alcoholic to come to his senses is, as I explained earlier, the sort of thing Satan would hope for and he has deluded almost everyone into thinking that's the best approach. To that I have only one question: Does it *work*?

It's time Christian people woke up to the fact that if they're willing to get involved, if they'll ask for and use My guidance in the matter, there'll be great strides made in putting an end to this tremendous problem of excessive drinking!

"Brethren, if a man be overtaken in a fault, ye which are spiritual, restore such an one in the spirit of meekness . . . Bear ye one another's burdens, and so fulfill the law of Christ." [1]

Waiting for the alcoholic to come to his senses when his senses are blotted out by booze is like standing quietly by hoping a blind man won't fall over the edge of a precipice when he's heading straight for it!

" . . . Take no part in the worthless pleasures of evil and darkness, but instead, *rebuke* and *expose* them." [2]

I ask you to love the alcoholic despite his actions—even as I have loved you. You've been hated, humiliated and harassed. You've been disappointed, depressed and discouraged. You've suffered hurts in your spirit, soul and perhaps body; but I'm asking you to forgive him even as I forgive you.

I ask you to exchange bitterness for compassion, hatred for love, and anger for gentleness and meekness of spirit.

I'm asking you not to argue, not to explain your actions unnecessarily, and not to be drawn into defending yourself against unwarranted accusations (because you'll get them). I'm asking you to abide in Me and I will pick up your defense.

---

1. Galatians 6:1-2.
2. Ephesians 5:11. (TLB)

I'm asking you to praise your loved one when he or she merits praise. I'm asking you to perform your duties to him or her and to your household regardless how you're treated because that's your responsibility, and " . . . inasmuch as ye have done it unto the least of these, My brethren, ye have done it unto Me." [1]

I'm asking you to have the mind which was in Christ Jesus and remember that he suffered unjustly at the hands of others. Yet he said, "Father, forgive them for they know not what they do." [2]

I want to stress forgiveness because it's a key to having your prayers answered. I state emphatically that you must forgive everyone who has hurt you or done anything wrong against you. If you can't remember all those people, call upon Me and I will bring them to your mind. Another message from My Word regarding forgiveness and answered prayer is this: "Therefore I tell you, whatever you ask in prayer, believe that you receive it and you will. And whenever you stand praying, forgive, if you have anything against anyone; so that I who am in heaven may forgive your trespasses." [3]

Have you forgiven the neighbor who made a slanderous remark about you?

---

1. Matthew 25:40.
2. Luke 23:34.
3. Mark 11:24-25.

Have you forgiven the youngsters who vandalized your premises? Have you forgiven that young son or daughter who disappointed you?

Have you forgiven that sales clerk who overcharged you and that bank teller who was rude to you? Have you forgiven that parent for neglecting you? For abusing you? Have you forgiven that driver who dented your fender in the parking lot and failed to report it to you?

Have you *truly* forgiven your alcoholic for all the hurt and grief and embarrassment he has caused you? *Have* you?

If not, you must. Remember, "Whatsoever ye shall bind on earth shall be bound in heaven: and whatsoever ye shall loose on earth shall be loosed in heaven." [1]

If you want to turn My power loose in your life, if you *really* want to see some action, start forgiving everyone! Now!

Remember, " . . . if you forgive men their trespasses, I will forgive you: but if you forgive not men their trespasses, neither will I forgive your trespasses." [2]

You can't forgive such seemingly gross injustices on your own. You don't have the power to do that. You have to call on Me to supply you with the grace to forgive, and My grace *is* sufficient for

---

1. Matthew 18:18.
2. Matthew 6:14-15.

the task. So abide in Me, forgive your alcoholic and pray. Keep your eyes focused on Me, not on your problem. You get a terribly distorted view, a frightening and ugly view, if you keep looking at that problem. Look to Me and be at peace.

Apart from Me you can do nothing. Apart from Me you can't forgive the alcoholic as I would have you forgive. Apart from Me, you can't love the alcoholic as I ask you to love him.

"This love of which I speak is slow to lose patience . . . it looks for a way of being constructive. (Do you have that kind of love?)

This love I speak of "is not possessive: it is neither anxious to impress nor does it cherish inflated ideas of its own importance. (Are you by chance being a martyr in your love for the alcoholic? Are you guilty of an inflated opinion of your role in caring for him? Do you wish to impress others with your longsuffering? Do you enjoy pity from others who say, "Poor Mary, she's having a hard time of things, yet look how she keeps on going"?)

The love I speak of "has good manners and does not pursue selfish advantage. It is not *touchy*. (Can you say that about your kind of love. Are you touchy? Does your alcoholic easily offend you?)

"It does not keep account of evil or gloat over the wickedness of other people. On the contrary, it is glad with all good men when truth prevails.

"Love knows no limit to its endurance, no end to its trust, no fading of its hope: it can outlast anything! It is, in fact, the one thing that still stands when all else has fallen." [1]

Can you say you have that kind of love for your alcoholic? If not, that's the kind for which you must strive, and you must use Christ as your example. When you can know that kind of love, there is *nothing* you can't overcome!

And what if you are buffeted for your love? For your suffering?

"A man does something valuable when he endures pain, as in the sight of God, though he knows he is suffering unjustly. After all, it is no credit to you if you are patient in bearing a punishment which you have richly deserved!

"But if you do your duty and are punished for it and can still accept it patiently, you are doing something worthwhile in My sight. Indeed, this is your calling.

"For Christ suffered for you and left you a personal example, and wants you to follow in His steps. He was guilty of no sin nor of the slightest prevarication, yet when he was insulted, he offered no insult in return. When he suffered he made no threats of revenge. HE SIMPLY COMMITTED HIS CAUSE TO THE ONE WHO JUDGES FAIRLY." [2]

---

1. I Corinthians 13:4-8.
2. I Peter 2:19-23.

He committed His cause to Me, and that's what I ask *you* to do.

Will your alcoholic be delivered?

" . . . if you live your life in Me, and My words live in your hearts, you can ask for whatever you like and it WILL COME TRUE FOR YOU!" [2]

" . . . believe on the Lord Jesus Christ, and thou shalt be saved, AND THY HOUSE!" [3]

I have given you My Word and My Word is truth. If you act upon it as I have commanded you, your alcoholic SHALL BE DELIVERED!

" . . . WITH GOD *ALL* THINGS ARE POSSIBLE!" [4]

Satan would have you be discouraged. I would have you be lifted up.

Satan would have you be afraid. I would have you be confident and without fear.

Satan would have you be angry and bitter.

I would have you be forgiving and compassionate.

Satan would have you mourn.

I would have you rejoice.

Satan would have you give up.

I would have you go on to the victory.

Satan would have you be tormented by your problems.

---

2. John 15:7.
3. Acts 16:31.
4. Mark 10:27.

I would have you be at peace, knowing I care for you, knowing I hear your prayers and knowing you can EXPECT ME TO ACT!

Satan will abandon you.

"I will be with you alway . . . even unto the end of the world." [1]

"CHOOSE YOU THIS DAY WHOM YOU SHALL SERVE." [2]

"BE OF GOOD CHEER: I HAVE OVER- COME THE WORLD!" [3]

---

1. Matthew 28:20.
2. Joshua 24:15.
3. John 16:33.

About the Author

Joyce Hartzell Hovelsrud was born and raised in southwestern Minnesota, received a BA degree from Sioux Falls College and did graduate work in theater and English at the Universities of Minnesota and South Dakota. She has been a high school and college English, speech and drama instructor, has directed for and acted in community and summer theaters, has been the head editor of a national magazine, and has managed the advertising agency for a major business enterprise in Denver, Colorado. As a free lance writer, she has authored greeting card gags and verse; self-help, inspirational and scholarly magazine articles; children's books, stories, films and plays, including a three-act musical; poetry; and television and film screenplays. She is the writer of *Holy Smokies*, a recent work relating the story of law officer Al Palmquist and the Midwest Challenge ministry. Joyce has recently moved from Denver to Minneapolis where she is currently acting in the capacity of editor-in-chief for Ark Books. She is the mother of two daughters: Angela, who lives in Sheridan, Wyoming; and Cynthia, who lives in Denver.

ARK BOOKS is owned and operated by MIDWEST CHALLENGE, INC., a non-profit Christian rehabilitation center dedicated to the restoration of lives ravaged by all kinds of drug abuse including alcohol.

The program is supported entirely by contributions, and those who wish to lend their support, to be placed on the mailing list and/or to inquire of its services may write to:

Midwest Challenge, Inc.
3049 Columbus Avenue South
Minneapolis, MN 55407

- -

If you have found this book helpful to you, won't you take the time to let us know about it? Fill in the blanks below and mail to Editor-in-Chief, ARK BOOKS, in care of the above address.

____ I have claimed my deliverance through Christ.

____ I have found victory over temptation.

____ Other _____

Your Name _____

Street Address _____

City_____ State _____ Zip_____

Other Good Selections from Ark Books

HOW TO LIVE WITH AN ALCOHOLIC AND WIN by Jim and Cyndy Hunt with Robert Allen Hill.—An in-depth work concerning the organizaton, Alcoholics Victorious: its founding, its beliefs and its methods. Included are lectures from a course of the same title by Jim and Cyndy Hunt, directors of the Minnesota Chapter; study guides; scripture references; the Seven Steps to Victory; and an appendix listing AV chapters throughout the United States and six foreign countries.

HOLY SMOKIES by Al Palmquist with Joyce Hovelsrud. Foreword by Billy Graham. —The thrilling story of preacher-cop Al Palmquist and other lawmen who deal with crime as per Christ's instructions 2,000 years ago. Clear-cut answers to the desperate crime-related problems confronting America today by the author of *The Minnesota Connection.*

WHAT'S IN A NAME? by Francis, Palmquist, Hartzell.—A unique collection of common names, both masculine and feminine. Each entry gives literal and spiritual meanings and an appropriate life-time scripture verse. One-of-a-kind in name reference books and an aid to counselors and prospective parents.

WHATEVER BECAME OF THE DRUG SCENE? by Al Palmquist.—It's far more insidious than people believe as this book explains. Also, a concise but thorough course in drug education and recommendations for what can be done. Especially appropriate for the older grade school child and the parent who would educate younger children before they encounter pressures from peer groups. Illustrated.

HOW TO SLAY THE DRAGON by G. Mark Denyes.—A collection of in-depth sermons on such topics as Ordinary Heroes, Seasons of the Soul, When Faith Fails, Gifts and Fruit and The Wonder of Worship. The old, old story related with fresh, new insight.

BIBLE NAMES by Francis, Palmquist, Hartzell.—A collection of Biblical names from Aaron to Zuriel. A handy reference for every student of God's Word and a must in every Christian library. Especially helpful to those prospective parents researching Bible names and meanings.

IT AIN'T NO DISEASE is soon to be released as a half-hour motion picture. For information write Box 26596, Mpls., MN 55426.